The Ultimate Guide to

Psychic Abilities

The Ultimate Guide to

Psychic Abilities

A Practical Guide to Developing Your Intuition

Karen Frazier

Illustrations by Roberta Orpwood

LEARN ABOUT

Clairvoyance
Mediumship
Channeling
Astral Projection
Precognition

FAIR WINDS

Inspiring | Educating | Creating | Entertaining

Brimming with creative inspiration, how-to projects, and useful information to enrich your everyday life, Quarto Knows is a favorite destination for those pursuing their interests and passions. Visit our site and dig deeper with our books into your area of interest: Quarto Creates, Quarto Cooks, Quarto Homes, Quarto Lives, Quarto Drives, Quarto Explores, Quarto Gifts, or Quarto Kids.

© 2021 Quarto Publishing Group USA Inc.
Text © 2021 Karen Frazier
Illustration © 2021 Roberta Orpwood

First Published in 2021 by Fair Winds Press, an imprint of The Quarto Group,
100 Cummings Center, Suite 265-D, Beverly, MA 01915, USA.
T (978) 282-9590 F (978) 283-2742 QuartoKnows.com

Fair Winds Press titles are also available at discount for retail, wholesale, promotional, and bulk purchase. For details, contact the Special Sales Manager by email at specialsales@quarto.com or by mail at The Quarto Group, Attn: Special Sales Manager, 100 Cummings Center, Suite 265-D, Beverly, MA 01915, USA.

25 24 23 22 21   1 2 3 4 5

ISBN: 978-0-7603-7139-8

Digital edition published in 2021
eISBN: 978-0-7603-7140-4

Library of Congress Cataloging-in-Publication Data

Names: Frazier, Karen (Karen S.) author.
Title: The ultimate guide to psychic abilities : a practical guide to
  developing your intuition / by Karen Frazier.
Description: Beverly, MA : Fair Winds Press, 2021. | Series: The ultimate
  guide to... | Includes index.
Identifiers: LCCN 2021004683 (print) | LCCN 2021004684 (ebook) | ISBN
  9780760371398 (trade paperback) | ISBN 9780760371404 (ebook)
Subjects: LCSH: Psychic ability. | Parapsychology. | Psychics.
Classification: LCC BF1031 .F7156 2021 (print) | LCC BF1031 (ebook) | DDC
  133.8--dc23
LC record available at https://lccn.loc.gov/2021004683
LC ebook record available at https://lccn.loc.gov/2021004684

Illustration: Roberta Orpwood

Printed in China

....

For Liz;
I'm incredibly proud of
your courage
in choosing to be who you are.

CONTENTS

• •

My Psychic Life

· ·

It's April 2, 1982, and I'm a sophomore in high school. It's the start of spring break, and my parents have packed up the car for a family road trip the next morning to the Bay Area. As I crawl into bed, my excitement over a trip to California is interrupted by a feeling of dread. One of my close friends, Dan, pops into my mind.

All night, I toss and turn, having nightmares about Dan. When I wake in the morning, my parents sit me down and tell me that overnight, Dan was killed by a drunk driver while he changed a friend's tire on the side of the freeway.

It's the spring of 1984, and I'm a college freshman living in the dorms at Eastern Washington University. One day as I get off the elevator in the dorm's lobby, I am overcome by a wave of terror. The image of my high school boyfriend, David, pops into my mind. We've been out of touch since I left for university in the fall, and I haven't spent much time thinking about him. So, it's odd that he came to my mind in association with this unexpected and seemingly unreasonable fear and anxiety I am suddenly feeling.

I try to shake it off and go about my day; after all, it's a warm, sunny Saturday, and I have big plans for my weekend. But the terror refuses to go away, always accompanied by thoughts of David. Finally, in the early afternoon, I'm so distracted I call him. It's the first time we've spoken in months.

"I know this is going to sound weird," I tell him. "But I've had this feeling all day, and I need to ask you about it. Are you planning to drive somewhere tonight?"

To my surprise, David answers in the affirmative. "I'm driving to Seattle tonight for a concert," he tells me.

It's a 90-mile drive (145 km) from our hometown along I-5 to Seattle, one I have made many times myself, but as David tells me this, another wave of fear washes over me.

"Don't go," I tell him. "I don't think you should go. I don't know why, but you cannot drive to Seattle tonight. Please don't." I realize I'm pleading, but I don't care. I am so overwhelmed with urgency as I talk to him that I can't help myself.

It takes a while because I can't explain to David why I feel the way I do, but eventually, he agrees to cancel his plans and stay home. That evening, there is a multiple-car pileup on the very stretch of I-5 he would have been driving.

It's 1994, and I'm living in Silverdale, Washington, on the Kitsap Peninsula. I'm preparing a meal for friends who are coming to dinner when I'm suddenly overcome with a deep sense of sadness. My beloved grandmother, Mary, comes to my mind. My telephone rings. When I answer, it's my grandfather, who tells me my grandmother has just died.

It's the summer of 1996, and I'm in my third trimester of pregnancy. For the past several months, I've been having vivid dreams about the baby. My due date is August

18, but I keep telling my midwife that I will have the baby on the 12th or 13th. I go into labor shortly before midnight on August 12, and my son is born early in the morning on August 13. He looks exactly like the baby I've been seeing in my dreams, and his temperament is the same as in my dreams.

It's December 2000. I am a recently divorced single mom who has just started working at a small, family-owned company in Everett, Washington. On my first day, the HR manager takes me around to meet the company's forty or so employees. When she introduces me to the tech support guy, Jim, he seems eerily familiar to me, but I can't place where I might know him from. He seems a bit odd, and I don't think I like him very much.

That night, I have an intense and hyperreal dream in which I am in a relationship with Jim. When I wake, all I can think is "Well, that's gross."

Over the course of the next several months, however, I get to know Jim and find I like him quite a lot. We are married in 2003.

It's February 2003. Jim and I have been married for about a week, and we're house hunting in Southwest Washington, where Jim has recently started a new job. We are both particularly drawn to one house in the small town of Chehalis that's about 5 miles (8 km) from where Jim works, and we put in an offer. It is quickly accepted.

Back home in our old house, after the offer has been accepted and earnest money paid, I have a vivid dream about our new home being haunted. Fortunately, I've convinced myself over the years that I don't believe in ghosts, so I shake off my dream and go about my life. I mostly forget about it as we move in and start our new life together as a blended family.

However, within a few months of living in the house, I notice increasingly weird things happening here. For example, one day I am sitting upstairs in my office while my six-year-old son, Tanner, is asleep in his bedroom downstairs and Jim is at work. I'm at my desk with my back to the door at the top of the stairs when I hear Tanner come up the steps and walk across the room. I'm intently focusing on my work and trying to finish writing a paragraph, so I don't turn around right away. As I finish writing, I feel Tanner bump the back of my chair, which spins slightly, and I can feel his breath on my ear. I turn to ask him why he's out of bed, and nobody is there. Surprised, I head downstairs and find Tanner still sound asleep in bed with our dog Spike curled up asleep next to him.

I've experienced incidents like these all of my life—times when I've simply known something I would have no way of knowing. What I didn't understand during any of these or the multitude of other incidents, however, was that I was receiving psychic messages. Even though these strange knowings had been with me since I was a young child, I never thought a lot about them because I didn't believe in psychic ability.

I grew up in the city of Bellingham, Washington, a town that sits just 20 miles (32 km) south of the Canadian border along the coast. My family was a church family; my dad was raised Catholic and my mom was a Protestant. Church and religion were important to us. I attended Sunday school every week with my sisters, and as a teen I was active in my church's youth group.

As the middle daughter of well-educated, religious parents, paranormal phenomena of any type simply weren't things I grew up believing were real. Regardless of the many strange and intuitive experiences I'd had all my young life, which included a number of "imaginary" friends, lots of strange knowings, powerful emotions that didn't seem to relate to anything going on in my life, and vivid and prescient dreams, it never occurred to me that psychic phenomena were real or natural.

I quickly learned these experiences weren't to be shared with others, and I believed they were simply part of being a creative kid with a vivid imagination. And yet, as I look back, I can easily recognize most of the experiences I had were likely the manifestation of psychic information that, because of my religious and educational upbringing, I had no idea how to deal with.

Today I understand differently. Over the past few decades, I've allowed myself to explore these intuitive gifts and work with them. I've overcome my societal and religious conditioning and chosen to lean into my psychic abilities instead of denying they exist. In fact, it seems strange to me today that I once had such difficulty understanding what was happening and why.

As I've gained literacy about psychic ability, which the world at large still considers a paranormal phenomenon, I've also started to recognize and understand the various ways it has been present throughout my entire life, from being a toddler and preschooler with imaginary friends all the way through adulthood when I became the person who was impossible to surprise (something my husband and kids absolutely hate) because I somehow just always know. I've come to understand all the ways I receive information, how psychic phenomena manifest, and how valuable it has been for my own mental and spiritual well-being to lean into my abilities instead of denying they exist.

I've also come to believe that everyone has the capacity to work with psychic ability because everybody receives intuitive information from the universe. It's just that our societal and religious conditioning has told us either that psychic ability isn't possible at all or that, if it is, it comes from a place of darkness instead of Light.

I believe differently. I know in the depths of my soul that not only is psychic ability natural, but it is of the Light. It exists as a sixth sense to enhance our five physical senses so we can receive guidance from the universe that serves our highest good if we are willing to allow that counsel into our lives. I also believe that every soul incarnated into a human body has access to this important guidance, but we often deny it exists because it is considered societally appropriate to do so.

Stepping into my own psychic ability has empowered me in many ways. When I was in denial about my psychic intuition, I suffered from significant anxiety. I often experienced tumultuous emotions that seemed unrelated to anything happening in my life, and I frequently worried there was something wrong with me. Denying my abilities caused me to struggle with the core of who I was. Accepting my abilities and working with them has brought me peace, joy, and comfort along with valuable guidance that has allowed me to step into my own personal power in ways I never dreamed possible. And you can experience these shifts in your life, too.

I'm reminded of an experience I had with my stepdaughter, Liz, when she was three. I was sitting in the car outside of a shop with Liz and Tanner as Jim ran inside to pick up something. From the back seat, Liz piped up with this: "Karen, this store is closed on Sundays!"

In front of us on the door of the store was a sign that read, "Closed Sundays."

Surprised, I turned around and looked at Liz. "Did you just read that?" I asked her.

She frowned at me and said, "Of course not. I'm only three. Everyone knows three-year-olds can't read."

And so it is with us. We believe we can't be psychic because there's a pervasive societal belief that psychic information is not real. Thus, while we may have knowings that we don't understand, we ignore them because we're only human, and everyone knows that humans aren't psychic.

Except that we are. I'm no different from anyone else. We all possess the ability to receive intuitive information. It may come in various forms from seemingly different sources, but the information is there for all who are willing to receive it, including you.

PART I

Understanding Psychic Ability

CHAPTER 1

Introduction to Psychic Abilities

· ·

Have you ever just *known* something? It might have been something simple that you didn't pay much attention to, such as thinking of someone a split second before you receive a call or text from them, or something more significant, such as suddenly knowing something is going to happen or having a dream about an incident that later occurs.

Every person's life is filled with these small, apparently random intuitive events. Most of us barely notice, and if we do pay attention, we explain away these experiences as coincidence or imagination. But what if they aren't? What if these seemingly random coincidences are actually manifestations of latent psychic ability that every incarnated soul on the planet possesses?

WHAT IS PSYCHIC ABILITY?

According to Merriam-Webster, *psychic* means "sensitive to nonphysical or supernatural forces and influences : marked by extraordinary or mysterious sensitivity, perception, or understanding." In other words, *psychic phenomena* are supernatural abilities that allow one to understand things without knowing how they are known, and *psychic ability* is possessing such capabilities.

The word itself is derived from the Greek word *psychikos*, which means "of the mind" and is related to the commonly used psychological term *psyche*, another Greek word that means "soul."

History provides many examples of psychic ability, including famous prophets, seers, astrologers, and more in various cultures throughout time, such as Ezekiel in the Bible; the Oracle of Delphi in classical Greece; French astrologer, physician, and prophet Michel de Nostredame (Nostradamus); twentieth-century American psychic and seer Edgar Cayce; and modern American psychic mediums James Van Praagh and Tyler Henry. Throughout history, some cultures have accepted that psychic abilities are natural and helpful, while others have deemed psychics to be charlatans and con artists or, worse, doing the work of the devil.

SUPERNATURAL OR NATURAL?

Many psychics, however, view this ability as completely normal and natural. Psychic information comes from Source, a web of interconnected energy that underpins the fabric of the universe. This is explained by the *resonance theory of consciousness*, which suggests that synchronized vibrations underlie all physical matter, including human consciousness.

Through the examination of quantum physics, the study of the smallest units of matter in the universe (subatomic particles), science has come to understand that all matter is made of tiny vibrating strands of energy held together by force fields to form the physical world we interact with. In other words, at the most basic level, everyone and everything you see and experience in our physical universe is made up of the exact same material: energy. And these micro bits of energy behave in ways that we may find incredibly strange from our observations of the physical world at a macro level.

Quantum physics is weird, even to quantum physicists, but it may hold the key to understanding psychic ability as a natural phenomenon. Science has shown that in the quantum world, objects often "sync up" when they are in proximity to one another, something discovered by Dutch physicist Christiaan Huygens in the 1600s. Sometimes called Huygens synchrony, this concept is more commonly known as *entrainment*.

Huygens placed two pendulums that were not in sync near each other on a wall. When he put them there, the pendulums weren't moving together. However, he observed that over time, they synched up and started to move in concert. This is a repeatable phenomenon that shows that when you place two objects vibrating at different frequencies near each other, they "lock into phase" and begin to vibrate at the same frequency.

Further, quantum physics has a principle that Einstein called "spooky action at a distance," something known more scientifically as *entanglement*. Experimentally, physicists have shown that when two subatomic particles become entangled, even after they have been separated by either time or distance, they remain entangled and therefore act in concert. The most common way this has been demonstrated is through spin, which is a type of quantum momentum. When entangled particles have been separated but remain under observation, experimentation has shown that when force is exerted to change the spin of one, the spin on the other changes instantaneously as well. This has been repeatedly demonstrated and even photographed.

So, what does all this science suggest about psychic ability? It suggests that the interconnection of all energy, including matter and consciousness, plays out in our daily lives.

The most widely accepted theory of the origin of the universe is the Big Bang Theory, which posits that the universe began as a small singularity that expanded to become everything we experience with our five physical senses today. Current theory suggests that all mass in the entire universe erupted from a single point in space that began to expand rapidly. Because all matter formed from this original point, it follows that all matter has been entangled since the formation of the universe and therefore remains entangled. From this entanglement, connections in consciousness may arise. In simpler terms, everything is connected, which makes it possible for the connection of human consciousness via psychic ability.

In this way, it's possible that science and metaphysics are moving toward the same understanding of the universe, but from different angles. It also suggests that, contrary to current societal beliefs, psychic ability is not a supernatural phenomenon but rather a manifestation of the natural laws of physics.

IS EVERYONE PSYCHIC?

If all human consciousness is entangled, it follows logically that all conscious humans have psychic abilities, or at least intuitive abilities. But if that's the case, then why isn't everyone talking to dead folks or winning the lottery week after week? The simple answer is that psychic information doesn't necessarily work that way, but the true answer is likely more complex.

- People may be ignoring or misidentifying psychic information because in many cultures and religions, there is a bias against psychic abilities and other phenomena deemed supernatural.

- Information manifests in different ways, some of them extremely subtle. Therefore, it can be easy to overlook the information or write it off as one's imagination.

- Often, psychic information is communicated symbolically using individual, familial, cultural, and collective symbolism that is difficult to understand.

- For some, psychic or intuitive information may be scary due to religious beliefs and the historical fear of people deemed seers, psychics, and witches.

THE DIFFERENCE BETWEEN INTUITION AND PSYCHIC INFORMATION

At their core, psychic information and intuitive information seem similar, if not the same. However, we tend to conflate intuition with instincts, which are ingrained patterns of behaviors inherent to every species, typically emerging due to their survival advantages. For instance, your "fight, flight, or freeze" response is an instinctual behavior that arises from responding to danger for the purposes of survival.

These instincts may be activated by *pattern recognition*, a subconscious understanding that certain circumstances may bring about outcomes that we need to instinctually react to. When our subconscious minds recognize these patterns, we may respond even before we are consciously aware of them.

Humans respond intuitively in many kinds of situations. For example, we often make a judgment about someone in the first few seconds after we meet them, something that forms as a gut feeling before we've even had the opportunity to evaluate our thoughts, feelings, and experiences with that person. We may feel or "just know" something is off with them before we have any information to support it. That knowing is your intuition.

Meanwhile, we often perceive what we deem psychic information as coming from a possibly supernatural outside source. It seems to arise mysteriously, often in dreams or visions.

However, it's likely that both psychic information and intuitive information arise from the same source and are the same energy, just experienced in different degrees or with different labels. Intuition is merely the more socially accepted form of psychic information, and both arise from the energetic field that underpins human consciousness and the entire universe. I tend to use both terms interchangeably because I believe they are both the same thing.

WHAT PSYCHIC ABILITY IS NOT

People have a number of misconceptions about psychic ability and what it is and isn't.

It Is Not Dark Magic

Because humans tend to fear what we don't understand, throughout history people have often feared those demonstrating psychic abilities. Historically, this caused many psychics to face religious persecution as witches—often with great personal consequences, including death. And while some psychics practice a form of spiritual paganism called Wicca, it's far from the dark witchcraft of fairy tales or the historical belief in evil witchcraft that led to executions throughout history. In fact, Wicca is a peaceful and helpful form of spiritual practice that involves working with the earth and elements to bring about positive change, not the dark or evil magic it was portrayed as being throughout history.

It Is Not Satanic or Demonic

Another fear-based response to psychic ability is labeling it satanic or demonic. This is especially prevalent among those practicing fundamentalist religions who believe the information psychics share doesn't come from God but rather from a dark source. And while some people working with psychic abilities may have darker intentions, most psychics you ask will tell you they believe the information they receive comes from the

Light of Source energy, God, or spirit guides. My beliefs and experiences indicate to me that the psychic information exists to help humans serve their greatest good. Therefore, I believe it is a gift from Source and is of the Light.

It Is Not a Way to Get Rich Quick

Perhaps the most frequent question I receive about psychic information is "If you're psychic, how come you can't psychically pick up what the lottery numbers are and win the jackpot?" In truth, I've never tried, nor do I think I ever would, for a few reasons. First, I don't really think psychic information works that way. I don't have a lot of control over the information I receive, and as far as I can tell, the universe has never tried to send me the lottery numbers (darn it anyway). Secondly, psychic information exists to serve the greatest good, and unless someone's greatest good is to win the lottery by receiving the winning numbers psychically, chances are you're not going to find a ton of people winning money this way. Can I categorically say this has never happened? Nope—perhaps it has happened that way, but if so, nobody's talking.

It Is Not a Form of Mind Control or Mind Reading

Several people have expressed to me, upon knowing that I am someone who works with my psychic gifts, "Don't try to read or control my mind." And while some people may want to use psychic information this way, once again, it doesn't necessarily work that way. Most of the psychics I know work within a strict code of ethics, and attempting to read someone's mind without their consent definitely falls outside of those principles. Likewise, no ethical psychic would ever attempt to use their abilities to control others, since many of us believe they are a gift that exists to benefit humanity.

It Is Not a Trick

At university, I used to amaze my friends at parties: someone would pop M&M's into my mouth one at a time while I was blindfolded, and I'd call out the colors of each candy I was tasting. This was a trick—I have a very sensitive palate and could taste the differences in the bitterness of the coating, which was an indicator of how much red dye it contained. I've also encountered so-called cold readers, who rely on mental tricks, subtle nonverbal cues, and creative questioning to appear to provide psychic readings. That is also a trick. Unfortunately, some people calling themselves psychics rely on fraud instead of genuinely trying to tune in to psychic information. But true psychic insight isn't a trick or a fraud. Instead, it's information that comes from Source to serve the greatest good.

PSYCHIC RESEARCH

While most people believe evidence of psychic phenomena is mostly anecdotal and therefore nonscientific, some scientists are conducting psychic research with promising results. *Parapsychology* is a social scientific discipline studying psychic ability (often called *psi*) and other phenomena. Many well-known institutions have been involved in parapsychological research using established social science protocols and scientific methods.

Gary Schwartz, University of Arizona

Gary Schwartz is a professor of psychology, medicine, neurology, psychiatry, and surgery at the University of Arizona. He has used triple-blind protocols to study consciousness, psychics and mediums, and other phenomena currently considered supernatural. The promising results of his increasingly rigorous studies have involved well-known psychics and mediums, such as Allison DuBois, as well as lesser-known people with psychic abilities. Schwartz's controlled studies have demonstrated that the psychic readers are receiving information at a statistically significant rate that exceeds chance.

Daryl Bem, Cornell University

Cornell University professor emeritus Daryl Bem has also studied psychic information in a controlled experiment using established social science protocols and scientific method. In 2011, he published his findings on precognition and premonition in the *Journal of Personality and Social Psychology*. His experiments, which used rigorous protocols, likewise appeared to prove psychic ability beyond statistical probability—

information that was so controversial in his field that it caused many social scientists to suggest there was something wrong with established social science protocols rather than accept his astounding results.

The Ganzfeld Protocol

Likewise, the *Ganzfeld protocol* appears to demonstrate the reality of extrasensory perception (ESP). Scientists use the protocol to induce episodes of spontaneous psi in subjects by reducing external stimulus, causing the brain to rely on internal imagery instead of sensory information. Meta-analysis of Ganzfeld protocol experiments conducted throughout the years shows beyond the instance of statistical probability—and, many believe, beyond a shadow of a doubt—that psychic phenomena do indeed exist.

THE U.S. GOVERNMENT AND PSYCHIC ABILITY

I have a friend who served in the CIA's and U.S. Army's Cold War psychic experiments, known as Project Stargate. The project started in the 1970s in a California lab and continued through 1995. During the project, psychics known as *remote viewers* (see page 59) were used to gain intelligence about America's enemies, including the Soviet Union. The remote viewers assisted in locating hostages, tracking down spies, espionage, and more. And while declassified documents show there was some success (and my friend reports there was a lot of success), critics suggest that any positive outcomes were coincidental. Still, the U.S. government threw a lot of money at Project Stargate for nearly two decades. And although the government spending money on something doesn't necessarily legitimize it, it certainly indicates someone felt it was worth the time, expense, and effort.

UNDERSTANDING PSYCHIC PHENOMENA

Research on psi remains ongoing. Independent researchers and organizations such as the Society for Psychical Research (SPR) and Institute of Noetic Sciences (IONS) continue to conduct experiments into the nature of psychic ability as well as the hows and whys of its existence and people's psychic capabilities.

And while psychic phenomena have historically been feared or discredited, there is a growing body of both anecdotal and scientific evidence that suggests it is a scientifically demonstrable phenomenon with a naturally explainable source. There's also a growing cultural curiosity about psychic phenomena and an increasing number of people who believe in them.

However, even with as many advances as we've seen in scientific protocols, understanding, and research, it's likely that we currently lack the technology to fully prove how and why psychic phenomena exist. Additionally, dogma, cultural beliefs, religious influences, and the presence of fraudulent psychics undermine the credibility of such evidence in the eyes of the public and much of the scientific community, making the study and understanding of psychic phenomena an uphill battle.

Nonetheless, many people have experienced intuitive hits, psychic awakening, or important prescient information from a psychic source. Many more could have these experiences if they understood how they received psychic information and how to use it to serve their own highest good. Moving forward with that goal, we'll discuss just how psychics perceive information and how to recognize whether you might be receiving it yourself.

CHAPTER 2

Recognizing Psychic Information

· ·

It took me a long time to understand how I could discern the difference between psychic information and my imagination. Often, psychic information is subtle, which is one reason so many people struggle to recognize or accept it. Additionally, the more someone suppresses or denies their abilities, the subtler or weaker they become. Think of it like a muscle: the more you exercise it, the stronger it becomes.

The first step in strengthening your psychic muscle is to learn to recognize when you may be perceiving psychic information using *clairs*, which are various forms of psychic sensory data. Next, you need to discern whether that information is coming from a psychic source or your imagination. By the end of this chapter, you'll have a much better idea how to do both.

HOW WE PERCEIVE PSYCHIC INFORMATION: UNDERSTANDING THE CLAIRS

It's important to understand the difference between how you *perceive* psychic information and how you *receive* it. You perceive psychic sensory information through the psychic senses—the *clairs*—which align with the physical, mental, and emotional senses. You receive psychic information through various manifestations of psychic ability that may involve these senses, such as touching an object (psychometry), or through the ways the information is perceived, such as mediumship and medical intuition, which are discussed in the next chapter.

When you perceive psychic information, it may be difficult to discern whether you're experiencing it with your physical senses or perceiving it with your psychic senses. For example, my friend Medea is clairaudient, meaning she receives information through psychic hearing. She used to think she simply had excellent hearing, believing what she heard came through her physical ears. However, with time, she came to recognize that the reason she could hear things that others couldn't is because she was hearing things with her psychic ears.

What's the difference? For many psychics, it's a subtle one. Some have such powerful psychic sensing abilities that they truly believe they are experiencing things with their physical senses. For example, I am *clairtangent*—that is, I sometimes experience psychic information as if someone is physically touching me. This most frequently occurs for me when the spirit of someone who has died is trying to get my attention so they can communicate with me through the other psychic senses.

I have these sensations frequently when I start to receive psychic information. I feel like someone is poking me on the shoulder, for instance, or stroking my cheek. However, the experience clearly doesn't arise from a physical encounter because I am a solid object and a spirit exists in energetic form and doesn't have a solid, physical finger to poke me or a hand to stroke me with. Therefore, the sensation of touch that I feel comes from an energetic exchange even though I perceive it as a physical one.

Likewise, when Medea hears psychic information, although she perceives it as the physical act of hearing, no solid, physical being or object is creating sound waves that physically strike her eardrums to create the physical experience of hearing. Rather, the information is being communicated to her via a nonphysical source that causes the section of her brain responsible for hearing (her auditory cortex) to receive the information as a sound even though it arises from pure energy.

There are multiple ways of psychically perceiving information. Some people use one or two of the clairs, while others may receive the information with more or even all of them. I have experienced all of them throughout my life.

In general, I've found that how you perceive psychic sensory input most strongly often coincides with how you best learn and process information. For example, if you are a visual person, you may process information best by looking at something, or you may have a flair for the other visual arts. In this case, your strongest method of perceiving psychic information may be clairvoyance (psychic seeing). If you love music and auditory input, you may be more apt to perceive psychic information through clairaudience (psychic hearing). If you are highly kinesthetic, you may perceive your information via clairtangence, and so on.

However, while most people do have one or two psychic senses that are the strongest, that doesn't mean the others won't show up for you. I've found with many of the psychics I've worked with that as they develop one of the clairs, the others start to fill in. Therefore, I always recommend that people remain open in order to let the information they need to receive to come to them in the best way possible.

Clairvoyance: Psychic Seeing

Clairvoyance is one of the best-known clairs. In fact, many people use the term to refer to any type of psychic ability. However, its meaning is more specific than is often found in general use.

Clairvoyance is most known as psychic seeing or clear seeing, and people with this form of psychic sensory perception often perceive psychic information through visual means. This can manifest in various ways.

Some people with clairvoyance perceive psychic imagery as a solid, physical presence that they actually seem to see with their eyes. For example, anyone who has ever seen a ghost or had a vision has experienced clairvoyance.

One of my experiences with clairvoyance occurred as I was in my early forties and reawakening to my psychic abilities. I'd become fascinated with a hiking trail that had been the site of an avalanche disaster, and I spent quite a bit of time at the location because I felt so drawn to it. One night, I was walking down the trail with one of my friends and saw the solid figure of a tall man shrouded in darkness. I asked my friend whether he saw the man, too, and as I asked, the man dissolved into nothingness. My friend hadn't seen him at all, but I was sure I'd seen him with my eyes.

This encounter couldn't have involved the physical act of seeing, however. First, I saw and perceived him as physical, but my friend who was standing right next to me didn't see him at all. Second, I saw the man dissolve, which isn't something you expect a physical human to do when you're staring right at him.

When we look at a physical object, light passes through our corneas, pupils, and lenses to hit the photoreceptors of our retinas. The retinas then turn this information into electrical signals that travel to the occipital lobe of the brain via the optic nerve. The result is vision.

However, nonphysical objects don't create the changes in light to send these signals to our brains through our eyes. With the man I saw, there was no physical stimulus there

to create the electrical signals that would lead to a sight experience. Instead, although I perceived the event in my mind's eye through clairvoyance, my experience made it seem as if I was seeing the man with my physical eyes while my friend, who was standing right next to me and looking in the same direction, didn't have the same experience. In other words, my visual experience was "all in my head" and not the result of something my physical eyes perceived.

Some people always have clairvoyant experiences in which they believe they are actually seeing physical objects with their eyes. Others, however, may only experience clairvoyant information in their mind's eye. For example, when I do a psychic reading, I often see flashes of images in my mind, which I can see with my eyes open or closed. These images may look like still photographs or short video-like snippets of visual information that flash through my mind so quickly I may miss them altogether if I'm not paying attention. Other times, they are more sustained still images or what appear to be longer video clips. In these cases, it feels more like I'm thinking in images rather

In addition to seeing images of objects or people, you might perceive clairvoyant information as any of the following:

- Objects that appear to float in and out of your field of vision (similar to an aura before a migraine)
- Colors in your mind or in your field of vision, including colors that surround people, animals, plants, or objects (Aura Reading—see page 66)
- Wavy or squiggly lines similar to heat haze
- Orbs or other light formations
- Numbers or symbols
- Flashes of light
- Varying textures, such as glitter or sparkling stars
- Fogs or mists
- Dark shadows
- Movement out of the corner of your eye

than seeing them with my eyeballs. When images are persistent and repetitive, that usually signals that it's something I need to pay attention to.

If you have a well-developed sense of clairvoyance, you may notice visual psychic information occurring in one or both ways: you may experience the information as if you are seeing things with your physical eyes and/or you may notice this information in your mind's eye. Both are equally valid clairvoyant experiences.

One of the best ways to strengthen your clairvoyance is by visualizing. It doesn't matter what you visualize—just close your eyes and create something in your mind's eye. Visualize as much detail as you possibly can, and hold the image for as long as you can. This strengthens your psychic clairvoyance muscle over time as your brain gets used to working with mental imagery. You can also use guided meditations involving visualization to help strengthen the visual facet of psychic perception.

Clairaudience: Psychic Hearing

I touched earlier on **clairaudience**, which is also called psychic hearing or clear hearing, when I discussed my friend Medea, who perceives psychic information most strongly through her sense of hearing.

When we hear with our physical ears, it is the result of something physical (such as striking a gong) creating sound waves. Those waves travel through the air, into the outer ear, and into the ear canal. The waves strike the eardrum, which vibrates in response, sending the signal to the bones of the middle ear, which vibrate to amplify the sound waves. From there, the amplified waves travel into the inner ear, causing vibration in the fluid there, which in turn transmits the vibration to various hairs in the inner ear that perceive sounds of all different frequencies and pitches. This creates an electrical signal that sends the sound vibration along the auditory nerve to the brain's auditory cortex (located in the temporal lobe), where we decode the vibration and experience it as a sound.

However, when we receive clairaudient information, there is no initiating physical action to create the sound waves that set off this cascade of events. In other words, nobody physically strikes a gong. Instead of the physical journey sound takes through the air, into our ears, and then into our brains, clairaudient information goes straight to our brains, even if we perceive it as an actual sound.

Just as with clairvoyance, individuals may believe they are hearing the sounds with their physical ears, or they may only hear the sound in their minds. I can give you examples of both.

One day on the same hiking trail I mentioned in the previous section, Jim and I were hiking with our friends Jayme and Bert. It was late in the afternoon on a weekday in September, so we were the only people on the trail. Part of the trail is covered with a huge concrete structure that was built as a snow shed to protect trains from avalanches, and we could see we were the only ones in the shed. As we walked back toward our cars through the snow shed, Jayme and I both heard a child's voice yell, "Hellloooo!" Neither Jim nor Bert heard it even though it was loud and quite clear to both Jayme and me. We heard the voice echo through the snow shed with the same acoustics as if someone had actually shouted in the concrete structure. However, our husbands both denied hearing anything, and there was nobody in the snow shed who could have yelled. It is likely that Jayme and I both perceived the voice via clairaudience even though it felt to us like we'd heard it with our physical ears.

On other occasions at the same location, friends have heard noises such as the sound of old-timey piano music, chatter, the sounds of a party, and people singing hymns. In most cases, a few people present hear this while others don't hear it at all.

On the other hand, I also sometimes hear clairaudient information just in my head. For example, I heard my father's voice in my head within a few hours of his death. I was sitting in the hotel room trying to process everything when I clearly noticed my father's voice in my mind. I was certain that it was wishful thinking since I was grieving powerfully after sitting with him as he died. I was clear, however, that what I was hearing was in my mind, much as if I had a song stuck in my head all day. I could hear the sound and cadence of his voice, but not what he was saying.

After a few moments of this, however, I heard my dad's voice say very loudly, "Listen to me!" At the same time, someone yanked on my hair lightly as if to get my attention. I took a deep breath and started to listen, and I then was able to focus on what my dad was telling me. He was excitedly describing what he was seeing and experiencing on "the other side." This was a very Dad thing to do; he was frequently excited and awed by new experiences and loved to share them with anyone who would listen. Throughout this entire encounter, though, I was easily able to discern that I was hearing him in my mind and not with my ears, which is why I originally believed it was wishful thinking and my imagination instead of a psychic experience.

Clairaudient information can be extremely clear, cohesive, and loud, or it may be much subtler. You may experience it as soft, barely there sounds, snippets of sound, or distant noises you can barely make out, as if you're hearing something off in the distance.

Whether you think you're hearing the sounds with your ears, in your mind, or both, clairaudient psychic sensory information may take the following forms:

- Music or snippets of music

- Isolated sounds from a musical instrument, such as drums, wind chimes, piano, gongs, or bells

- Voices sharing words, phrases, or syllables, either in a language you speak or one you don't recognize

- Whispering

- Vocalizations such as laughter, chanting, singing, shouting, or crying

- Other human sounds, such as singing, sniffing, sneezing, or coughing

- Percussive noises, such as footsteps, shuffling, or knocking

- Sounds of nature, such as ocean waves, a babbling brook, softly blowing wind, animal vocalizations, or the rustling of leaves

- Whooshing or crackling noises

- High-pitched squealing or ringing, similar to the ringing experienced in tinnitus

- A voice or noise that wakes you from sound sleep

- A sense of pressure on your eardrums, similar to when your ears pop on an airplane, or the dampening or amplifying of sound for no discernible reason

You can assume the above sounds are clairaudient if there is no physical stimulus that would create such auditory sensations. For example, one morning I was sound asleep when I was awakened by the sound of a singing bowl ringing. I'm a sound healer, so I have lots of singing bowls in my house, but I was home alone, and nobody was playing any of them. Even after I was fully awake, the singing bowl continued to ring. In the absence of a physical reason for the sound, I could only assume I had been awakened by a clairaudient experience.

You can strengthen your clairaudient abilities by using your auditory imagination. Close your eyes and try to hear a song playing in your head. Imagine different sounds, such as musical instruments, dog barks, and more. Regularly using your imagination in this way can help fortify clairaudient abilities.

Clairtangency: Psychic Touch

Clairtangency is known as psychic touch or clear touch and involves sensing physical touch in the absence of physical stimulus. If you are clairtangent, you may feel the sensations of physical touch as if it is actually happening, or you may perceive that you are being physically touched in your mind even if you realize it isn't actually happening physically.

We perceive the sense of touch through nerves and receptors in our skin, known as the *somatosensory system*. These receptors send signals to our brains that help us perceive hot, cold, wet, dry, pressure, pain, and more. A healthy somatosensory system typically requires a physical stimulus to produce a physical sensation.

However, we can also perceive these apparent physical sensations psychically through a clairtangent experience. In these cases, it's often clear there is no physical stimulus to create the sensation. This type of psychic perception can be among the more difficult to discern, however, because due to the way our somatosensory system works, there can be other physical causes for feeling as if we've received physical touch information, such as muscle twitches that cause us to feel like someone is poking us, nerve misfires that result in pain in the absence of physical stimulation, or hot flashes caused by hormones.

Therefore, if you feel you're having clairtangent experiences, it's always best to check with your primary health care provider first to make sure there's not a physical condition causing the sensations.

I mentioned earlier that I tend to have clairtangent experiences rather frequently. This is because I've always been a kinesthetic person—someone who learns best by doing and experiencing. I prefer to learn a new task by experiencing it in a touch-based way over any other form of learning. Therefore, I can provide a quick example of a physical sensation I have that's a clairtangent experience.

I'll start by mentioning that I am a woman of a certain age. I've been experiencing menopause and all of the joy that comes with that life transition, including hot flashes. Therefore, I know what a hormonally driven hot flash feels like in my body. For me, it always starts in my midback and extends upward and downward, first along my back and then creeping throughout my entire body.

However, I also sometimes experience hot flashes when I'm working with someone in an energy-healing environment. I have a friend, Kasci, whom I call a Reiki sponge because when I channel energy to her through Reiki or work with another energy-healing modality, I always experience an instantaneous full-body hot flash as soon as I lay my hands on her. I've had this experience with other energy-healing clients, too, and I interpret it as a signal that they really need the energy I'm providing. As I channel the energy to them, the heat eases. This is a form of a clairtangent experience.

In the course of working with my energy healing clients—whom I prefer to call healing partners because they are active in their own healing and care—I also frequently feel sensations in my body or my hands that tell me where the person needs me to channel the energy. For instance, my hands may feel cold when I place them over the pancreas of someone with diabetes, or I may experience a pain in my shoulder if I'm working with a healing partner who has a shoulder injury. These are all examples of clairtangent information, as is the experience I relayed earlier about feeling my recently deceased father yanking on my hair.

I frequently perceive communication in the form of clairtangency when I am performing a psychic reading, particularly when I am working as a medium and communicating with someone who has died. For instance, I was once doing a walk-through of a client's home. The client thought her house was haunted and wanted me to see what I could do about the energy there. As I walked into her bedroom, I felt a sudden and intense physical sensation that I can best describe as vertigo. I got a severe headache the second I entered the room; then, the room spun three times around me, and everything went black as I felt the sensation of my body hitting the floor—even though I was still on my feet. This happened three separate times as I stepped in and out of the room to verify my experience. Once I was certain of what I was sensing, I told my client what I had experienced. She told me her mother had stepped into

Some ways one might perceive clairtangent information include:

- Hot or cold spots despite the temperature where you are being consistent

- Sensations such as someone poking you, pulling your hair, or stroking your skin

- Itchy skin with no apparent source

- Pushing, pulling, tingling, pressure, heat, or cold

- Feeling as if someone is nearby, such as feeling a prickling sensation like someone is watching you or physically feeling a mattress depress as if someone is sitting down on it next to you

- Vertigo or hot flashes

- Changes in your proprioception (the sensation of where your body is in space), such as feeling as if the earth is moving under your feet or feeling like you're floating even when you're standing on solid ground

that room, had a stroke, and died there. My clairtangent experience was the sensory representation of what her mom had experienced. As soon as I left the house, all of the physical sensations I'd had while I was there resolved.

Because I experience clairtangency so frequently and use it so much in my work as a psychic and energy healer, I've become adept at discerning whether a sensation is something I'm physically experiencing or psychic information. When I do have trouble discerning, however, I close my eyes and ask, "Is this mine?" Then, I wait for a sensation that gives me an answer.

Clairtangency can be disturbing when you don't recognize what you're dealing with. However, I find it useful in my psychic and energy-healing work, even though it can be a little difficult on my body. I've found that the best way to keep myself protected is to note the information I've received, thank the source providing it, and then visualize a shower of white light pouring into my head and down through my body, pushing the physical sensations out through my feet and into the earth. This almost always helps.

Clairolfactance: Psychic Smelling

Clairolfactance is also known as psychic smelling or clear smelling. It is when you smell something, but there's nothing there that would make it smell that way. It's actually one of the most common forms of psychic sensory perception, although most people don't recognize it as such. As with all of the other clairs, you may experience clairolfactance as if you are actually smelling something with your physical nose, you may only perceive the aroma of something in your mind, or you may experience a combination of the two.

I used to volunteer at the local history museum, which is a well-known haunted hot spot in my town. One of the experiences many employees and guests on paranormal tours have reported there is smelling the aroma of a floral perfume in the museum's attic, which is a storage space. I've smelled it myself on several occasions, and it moves through the attic, appearing in random places. In my time at the museum, I searched the attic high and low but never discovered an apparent physical source for the aroma.

Your sense of smell is one of your chemical senses. You have smell receptors inside your nose called olfactory sensory neurons. As you breathe, molecules strike those neurons, which carry signals to the olfactory cortex in your brain's temporal lobe, where the smell is interpreted. As with the other senses, the physical sense of smell requires the presence of physical molecules to start the process.

However, if you have a clairolfactant experience, there is no physical molecule that connects with your smell receptors, but you still perceive an aroma. And while there can be physical causes for this that require medical attention, it can also arise from psychic sources. In that case, the physical system is bypassed, and the perception of smell comes entirely from clairolfactance.

One of the primary ways I experience clairolfactance is that I smell the aroma of ozone just before I begin to receive other psychic information. This appears to be one of the signals I receive through my sense of smell to pay attention to further information arriving through my other psychic senses.

Some common aromas people smell through clairolfactance include:

- Flowers
- Perfume
- Smoke
- Food
- Petrichor (the smell of the first rain after a dry spell)
- Ozone or other atmospheric odors
- Decay

In my experience, clairolfactance tends to be more of a signaling psychic sense versus one that imparts a ton of information, although some psychics I know also receive smells as information to impart to their clients. For example, when one of my psychic friends performs gallery readings, he frequently shares his perception of aromas as he reads a specific spirit.

If you'd like to develop your sense of clairolfactance, close your eyes and bring to mind powerful smells you associate with good memories, such as the aroma of your favorite flower, the way a parent smells or smelled, or the scent of freshly baked bread.

Clairgustance: Psychic Tasting

Clairgustance is also known as psychic tasting or clear tasting. It is closely linked to clairolfactance, since smell is involved in the sensation of taste, and it's another of your chemical senses.

Your tongue is equipped with taste buds that can sense sweet, sour, bitter, salty, and umami (savory). Along with the taste buds on your tongue perceiving these basic flavors, the aromas from what you eat travel up into your nasal passages so you can interpret the flavors of the food, which come from the molecules in it. There is also the component of texture involved in taste that makes eating a unique sensory experience. Ultimately, however, when you eat or drink something, that sensory experience occurs because of your body's interaction with the chemical molecules that make up the food or beverage.

With clairgustance, you may notice tastes in your mouth when you aren't eating any food. Instead, you're perceiving psychic information using your sense of taste. For example, one of my psychic medium friends perceives the taste of blood in her mouth whenever she is communicating with a spirit that has died a sudden, accidental death or died through homicide.

Common tastes associated with clairgustance include:

- Metal
- Blood
- Wine, beer, or other alcoholic beverages
- Food flavors
- Bile
- Chemical tastes

As with your other psychic senses, you can develop your clairgustance by using your imagination. Close your eyes and minimize other physical sensory input. Then, try to imagine the tastes of some of your favorite foods as clearly as you can.

Clairsentience: Psychic Sensing

Clairsentience is also known as psychic feeling or clear feeling. It's feeling psychic information through sensory input not otherwise described by the basic five physical senses of sight, sound, touch, taste, and smell—I like to define it as the ability to pick up "vibes."

I've always been highly clairsentient. Even when I was a kid, I noticed that people, places, objects, and situations all had a unique "feel" to me, each different from the others. So even if I was in a room with my back to the entrance when someone I knew walked in without speaking, I'd always be able to sense who was there without seeing or hearing them. As a kid and young adult, when I lacked the vocabulary to express what this was, I simply called it their "vibe" or their "energy signature."

Perhaps the easiest way to understand the psychic sensory experience of clairsentience is to visualize someone you love deeply and spend a lot of time with. Close your eyes and invoke their presence in your mind. Do they "feel" a certain way? Now, invoke the presence of someone you know well but don't like very much. How do they feel? Notice the difference in feel between one and the other. This is their vibe.

I've always identified clairsentience as a psychic "first impression," sort of an instinctive hit that allows you to take measure of a person, place, object, animal, plant, or situation before your brain has had the opportunity to evaluate it.

Clairsentience may arise in various ways, including:

- Walking into a room and immediately feeling whether the energy is positive and upbeat or negative and awkward

- Feeling a sense of foreboding or danger when there isn't any source of danger clearly present

- Experiencing the feeling of a particular person just before you receive a text or call from them

- Knowing the type of mood someone is in without any physical indications of that mood

- Knowing someone is watching you even though your back is to them

- An instantaneous sensation that something will be negative or positive

- Getting goosebumps when the energy changes in a space

To strengthen clairsentience, pay attention to your first impressions. If you notice the feel of something, make note and then see how your logical thoughts stack up to that initial impression.

Claircognizance: Psychic Knowing

Claircognizance is known as psychic knowing or clear knowing. It's like receiving a psychic download of information: one moment you don't know anything about something, and the next minute you know everything, even though you haven't received any outside information to tell you about it.

For example, I had a new client who asked me to come to her house a few years after her husband had died. I didn't know anything about the client or her husband other than her name and address. So, I headed out with my bodyguard in tow (okay, husband—I don't go to strangers' houses alone) and went to her home. When I walked in, I immediately knew that her husband had been a cop or firefighter (I felt he had "cop energy"), that he sat in a chair near the front door, and how he had died. I knew all this the minute I walked through her front door, and when I relayed that information to her, it turned out I was correct: he was a firefighter, the chair by the front door was his favorite seat, and my information about how he had died was correct.

Claircognizance is the main way I perceive psychic information. I've been able to identify the history of places, known things about people's lives and deaths, and more simply by stepping into a space. It's a weird sensation to not know something and then suddenly know it, but for me and many others, it seems to be how the psychic thing works.

Claircognizance is best used in conjunction with the other psychic senses. When I'm hit with a "download" of information, I often ask for other sensory information to verify, and from there I can begin sharing information with my clients.

The best way to strengthen claircognizance is to work with it. When you suddenly know something you didn't before, don't ignore it or assume it's your imagination. Write it down or record it in some other way, and then seek to verify it through other psychic information, by asking people, or by conducting your own research.

Clairempathy: Psychic Feeling

Clairempathy, which may simply be called empathy or being an empath, is the ability to experience others' emotions as if they are your own. For many, it can be a difficult gift to have until they learn various ways to work with it and protect themselves. (See chapter 7 for coping strategies for empaths.)

I am highly empathic and have been all of my life. Before I understood that I was empathic, I often thought there was something wrong with my mental health because my emotions were all over the place regardless of anything that was happening in my life, and I seemingly had little control over them. As a result, I experienced a great deal of anxiety, something my mother confirms I had when I popped out of the womb.

I use empathy to my clients' and healing partners' advantage in my work as a psychic and energy healer because I experience their emotional states as if they are my own. This allows me to help them work through their own feelings and emotions, although I've had to learn over the years not to take on their emotions.

One of the best ways to learn to work with empathic information is to first recognize it when it occurs. Some signs you might be empathic:

- Your emotions are all over the place whenever you're someplace crowded

- You have deep emotions that don't seem to relate to what's going on in your life

- You struggle with anxiety or depression

- When someone else cries, you cry

- You feel much calmer when you're alone than when you're out among other people

- It pains you deeply to hurt someone's feelings, even unintentionally

- You always want to help people and animals that are hurting

- You have trouble observing any type of violence, even fictional or sports-related violence

- When someone in your orbit doesn't feel well, you don't either

- You can tell when someone is being untruthful

- You feel deeply connected to plants, animals, or the earth and can pick up on when they are ill

It can be difficult if you are empathic to discern whether what you are feeling belongs to you or someone else, so when you notice an emotion that seems out of place, go within and see whether you can connect it to something that's happening in your life. If not, it may be unrelated to you at all.

If you think you might empathic, complete the self-assessment in chapter 7.

IS IT IMAGINATION OR PSYCHIC INFORMATION?

You may have noticed as we discussed the various clairs that I mention frequently it may be difficult to discern psychic information from your imagination. Even seasoned working psychics struggle with this, which is one of the reasons no psychic is ever 100 percent accurate (and why you might want to look elsewhere for psychic assistance if you encounter one who claims they are).

So how can you discern whether you are receiving psychic information or it's your imagination? It's not an exact science, but there are some clues that can help you decide. If it's psychic information, you may notice some of the following:

- The information is persistent or recurrent; it doesn't go away over time or repeats on a loop until you pay attention to it

- The information comes suddenly or instantaneously without you having to think about it—it seems to come out of nowhere

- The input is verifiable—you can fact-check the information and discover it is true

- It feels right; you experience a strong sense of resonance

- The information is helpful or serves the greater good

- Impressions you receive are extremely vivid

- The information is entirely novel

- The information may seem impersonal or emotionless (to you) but still somehow important

With the exception of empathic information, psychic information is generally nonemotional and persistent. It may feel like a "gut" feeling: you know it's important and real, but you don't know how you know, and it's often unrelated to anything occurring in your life.

* *

With knowledge of how you perceive psychic information and some tools to discern that information from your imagination or wishful thinking, it's time to look at the various ways you can receive psychic information.

CHAPTER 3

Manifestations of Psychic Ability

·······································

A long with the clairs discussed in the previous chapter, which indicate how you *perceive* psychic messages, it is also helpful to understand the various ways you might *receive* psychic information. I call these "manifestations" of psychic ability, and everyone has their own unique ways that they receive the psychic-sensory information that arrives via the clairs.

For example, my husband, Jim, used to declare, "I am about as psychic as a rock." However, that man has an uncanny sense of direction. Plop him down in the middle of someplace he's never been, and he can navigate his way out of it without using a map, GPS, a compass, or any other tool. Since I am exactly the opposite—I could get lost in my own bed and couldn't navigate my way out of a paper bag—I've always been curious about how he does this. I asked him how he managed such an amazing trick.

Jim explained that it's part a sense, part a knowing, and part actually seeing in his mind a three-dimensional map overlaying his thoughts and the landscape that allows him to get where he needs to go without getting lost and without outside help. In other words, Jim perceives the information as a visualization (clairvoyance) and a feeling (clairsentience) or knowing (claircognizance), and he receives it through the manifestation of an uncanny sense of direction. It turns out Jim is probably a little more psychic than a rock—no offense to rocks. Jim's ability is a form of geosensitivity, one of the many manifestations of psychic ability that we'll look at in this chapter.

MEDIUMSHIP

The movie *The Sixth Sense* provided mediums a way to describe what we do: "I see dead people." A clairvoyant psychic medium can, indeed, see dead people—or the things dead people want them to see. Of course, not all mediums are clairvoyant, so some communicate with people who have died using their other psychic senses.

Mediumship is the ability to communicate with people who have died using psychic perception. Mediums serve as intermediaries between souls in the spirit world and the living. All mediums are psychic, but not all psychics are mediums. Mediums tend get more attention than other psychics, however, because many people find comfort in the ability to communicate with loved ones who have died.

A majority of the psychics who appear on television, such as John Edward, Theresa Caputo, and Tyler Henry, are psychic mediums who help people connect with dead loved ones. They often bring messages of comfort and hope from the other side to help people heal after the death of a loved one.

I am a medium myself and have had many experiences communicating with people who have died. This communication with spirits has changed my perception of death; I'm no longer fearful of dying because I know life goes on after we leave our physical bodies. It is also my experience that communicating with someone who has died provides deep healing and comfort for those left grieving their loss.

Dead loved ones don't always come through in the readings I provide, but they often do, sometimes even before I've started the reading. It seems that the souls of people on the other side know when their loved ones who are still embodied (see page 36) are about to attempt communication, and they're eager to make their messages heard.

A medium never knows who's going to come through, however, so if you're going to visit a medium, it's best to leave expectations at home. Many people come to mediums hoping to speak to a certain person, but there's no guarantee that's who is going to pop in. I've communicated with as many great-great-great-grandparents, distant relatives, pets, and friends of friends as I have with people who had much closer relationships to the individual receiving the reading.

Often the information I receive is cryptic or symbolic. Sometimes it's literal. Sometimes it communicates important messages. Sometimes it imparts messages of love and healing. Sometimes it simply provides confirmation that a loved one is on the other side and watching over those still living. Sometimes what seems nonsensical to me is deeply meaningful to my client. I know it's not up to me to translate the information I receive—my job is to impart the information exactly as I receive it and allow the person requesting the reading to interpret what it means.

This can sometimes be a bit awkward. For example, I was once communicating with a client's brother, who had died while she was still a teen. I described to her the information I received: long, wavy dark hair pulled back into a ponytail, torn jeans with motorcycle boots, pale skin, blue eyes, round John Lennon glasses, and a mustache. But every time I focused on the mustache, the word *pornstache* popped into my mind. Since I try my best to avoid upsetting my clients, there was no way I was going to use that word to describe her dearly departed brother.

Instead, I kept saying things such as, "He has this super-thick, handlebar-type mustache," which is my interpretation of what "pornstache" would indicate. My client kept responding with, "Well no, he had a mustache, but it wasn't very long or thick." We went around like this a few times before I heard very distinctly in my mind, "Say 'pornstache.'"

Against my better judgment, I said, "He's telling me to say 'pornstache.'"

My client burst out laughing and said, "Oh yeah—that's him."

It turns out her brother used to joke that if he could grow a mustache as thick as his sister's hair, he'd have a real pornstache. My using that word, which I was so hesitant to include, was the confirmation she needed to let her know it was, indeed, her brother. It was a reminder to share the exact information I receive with my clients instead of trying to censor it.

In another reading with the same client, I kept hearing her mother say "Beano," but I assumed it must be my imagination—why on earth would Beano be important unless someone was super gassy? The information kept repeating, however, and finally I said to her, "She keeps saying 'Beano.'" It turned out my client, whose name was Robyn, had been nicknamed Robeano as a kid, and it was what her mother called her.

Mediumship readings can be confusing for the reader because while some spirits just start talking to you like a living person would, most communicate through symbols, physical sensations, important verifications, images, events, and other references. I've found that because of this, it's pointless to try and interpret information myself; I leave that part to the client.

Another issue in medium readings is that sometimes multiple spirits come through together, piggybacking on one another, and it's difficult to make out which messages are coming from whom. In that case, a medium simply relays all of the information as it is received and lets the client sort out who is trying to convey what information.

Mediumship is a psychic gift that often scares people because death is a great unknown. However, for people grieving the loss of a loved one and the mediums who are sharing messages of hope, the impact of a reading can be life-changing. What's important is that both the medium and the client approach it with a sense of openness to whichever spirits and whatever messages come through. You never know who will come through in a medium reading, nor what the spirits will convey. But the spirits who communicate with and through mediums usually do so to serve the highest and greatest good.

TELEPATHY

Telepathy is also known as mind reading because people who are able to practice telepathy can read what's in someone else's mind and communicate using their own thoughts. It is often portrayed in movies and television as two people staring intently at one another and reading each other's thoughts (usually with subtitles or voiceover). However, in truth, telepathy comes through the same channels of perception as all other psychic gifts. So, the person receiving the information (the reader) may perceive it via any of the clairs. The information may come in the form of the exact words and thoughts in another's mind or in the various other forms of sensory psychic perception.

Likewise, the person whose mind is being "read" (the sender) will be sharing any information in their mind in the manner through which they best process information. A visual sender might be thinking of their first car and seeing it as a picture in their mind, while an auditory receiver may perceive the words "Chevy Nova" instead of seeing the image of the car. Therefore, if you practice telepathy using one of the exercises we'll discuss in chapter 6, be aware that regardless of how a sender is visualizing the information, you may perceive it differently.

The reason this likely happens is that, like all matter in the universe, information is vibration. How we perceive that energy when we receive it is related to how our individual brains are wired. So, in the psychic space, it's perfectly natural for our brains to decode energy in the ways it best processes information.

Jim and I seem to share some natural telepathy; it's something we both noticed early in our relationship, and it has grown stronger the longer we've been together. However, our brains are wired differently. I'm the creative, wispy, woo-woo chick who is rarely grounded and often speaks and thinks in symbols, while he's more concrete, grounded, and linear. Therefore, his thought processes are much more concrete than mine. Still, we manage to link telepathically.

For example, late last year, I started to feel pain in my chest, and I felt a growing uneasiness about my husband's health. I kept asking Jim, who has coronary artery disease and has had a few angioplasties, whether everything was okay. He kept reassuring me all was well, but the uneasiness wouldn't go away.

We were on vacation in Canada when he told me he was having chest pains. It turned out he'd been having them from essentially the moment I started asking him about them, but he'd been hoping they would pass, and he didn't want to worry me. A week after we returned from our vacation, he had another angioplasty and stent placement. He had been communicating the information with me telepathically, even though his words said something different.

I suspect many people have small experiences of telepathy daily but don't recognize them as such. The information may occur quickly and subtly as a thought flash or, like my experience with Jim's coronary artery disease, it may be stronger and more sustained. However, we are conditioned to believe these instances are imagination or coincidence, so many people don't recognize that they are receiving and communicating telepathic information regularly.

REMOTE VIEWING

While many people confuse this manifestation with telepathy, they are two different things. **Remote viewing** is a protocol through which people with psychic abilities visualize a place, person, or object that is somewhere else.

As mentioned in chapter 1, the U.S. government worked with remote viewers in its experimentations with psychic intelligence as a form of espionage. Think of it like a spy satellite, only instead of an object launched into space, it involves the human mind and psychic perception. Or like watching a psychic television.

I have a few friends who worked with the U.S. military and CIA remote viewing protocols. Anyone can learn these protocols, although some people remote-view naturally as a by-product of their psychic abilities. The government allegedly employed people who were able to demonstrate these skills using the protocols to gain insight into governments the US deemed enemies of the state as a form of psychic espionage.

My grandmother was a remote viewer, although as a staunch and proper Catholic, she never would have described it this way. My grandma loved Christmas; every year, I'd come into the living room and find her under the Christmas tree touching packages. As she touched each one, she'd say what she thought was in it. She always nailed it. It was both amusing and challenging—you couldn't surprise grandma with a gift, no matter how hard you tried.

Much to my family's frustration, I have inherited this gift, so I'm also notoriously difficult to surprise. The best way to keep me from knowing what's in a gift is put it somewhere I can't find it until it's time to open it. Otherwise, as soon as I see the gift, without even trying, what's inside pops into my mind. This usually manifests as an image of the object, but occasionally it's just a knowing or the words that describe the object. For example, once Jim gave me a wrapped gift, and as soon as I saw it, the name Le Creuset—a popular brand of enameled cast iron pots—popped into my mind. When I opened the gift, I saw it was a sunset-colored Dutch oven. On another occasion, he bought me a red leather jacket, and as soon as I saw the package, I saw the exact jacket in my mind's eye.

If you sometimes see images in your mind of people you've never met or places you've never been, you may be using your powers of clairvoyance to remote-view.

PRECOGNITION

Precognition occurs when you know something is going to happen before it does. Sometimes, people with precognitive abilities are called *precogs* or *seers*.

I have precognitive abilities connected to different types of events, including earthquakes and train derailments. Unfortunately, I'm helpless to do anything about any of these events; I'll receive the information that something is imminent through one of my clairs, but I won't receive specifics about where, when, why, who, or how. This can be quite frustrating, but I've come to understand that all I can do when I receive precognitive information is to send loving energy to the planet and to anyone who might be affected by what I've seen.

Well-known prophets such as Michel de Nostredame (Nostradamus) and Edgar Cayce (the Sleeping Prophet) most likely had the gift of precognition. In the sixteenth century, Nostradamus predicted a number of world events far in the future, including the rise to power of Napoleon and Hitler and possibly the September 11, 2001, terrorist attacks. Cayce, who received his information while in a deep meditative state, appears to have predicted such major world events as the 1929 stock market crash, World War II, and various atmospheric events and natural disasters.

Precognition may arise in a few different forms, and it can come to the person receiving the information via any of the psychic senses.

Precognitive Dreaming

Precognitive dreaming is when someone receives future information through the language of dreams. Dreams tend to be symbolic, but dream interpretation (see chapter 5) can help you to decode what your nighttime meanderings tell you. Sometimes the precognitive information that comes in dreams is symbolic, but at other times it is literal.

For example, my precognition about train derailments always comes in dream form. Instead of being symbolic, however, the dreams are intense and literal. I see the event as if I am watching it with my waking eyes. These dreams often have a hyperreal quality—in other words, they seem even more vivid than reality. Many people who have precognitive dreams have shared similar experiences with me. Typically, my precognitive dream comes to me twenty-four hours or less before the actual event, but people may have dreams days, weeks, or even years in advance, making them more difficult to confirm. For this reason, if you believe you're having precognitive dreams, I recommend you keep a dream journal so you can look back and connect the dots.

Precognitive dreams may also be symbolic. For example, recently I came across a journal containing a dream I'd had more than two decades ago. In the dream, I found myself in a house filled with crystals of all sizes, colors, and shapes. I was absolutely delighted by my finds. At the time, I didn't own any crystals. About ten years later, my lifelong interest in crystals was reignited, and I started studying and writing about them. I've now written four books about crystals, my house is filled with them, and I use them daily both in personal practices and in my energy healing and psychic work. It was surprising how closely a twenty-year-old dream I'd forgotten aligned with my life today.

Premonitions

Premonitions are another form of precognition in which you suddenly have a feeling or a knowing about some event before it happens. The feeling I had about my high school boyfriend driving to Seattle, mentioned in the introduction, is an example of a premonition. I didn't understand exactly what would happen; I only knew I needed to ask him not to drive to Seattle. It was a nonspecific feeling, or vibe, that caused me to act.

I've learned to trust these feelings and act on them. If something doesn't feel right to me, if the vibe is off, then I change my plans accordingly. I don't know what, if anything, this has spared me from experiencing, but I realize I receive such information for a reason, and I always respect it.

You can receive a premonition through any of your clairs—whether it's simply a vibe or something much more concrete, such as a vision.

RETROCOGNITION

Retrocognition is the flip side of precognition: it's the ability to perceive information from the past.

Occasionally, I've walked into a location and immediately known its history even though I've never been there before and knew nothing about it. For instance, once I went to a client's home because there was a weird kind of juju there that was frightening them. As soon as I stepped onto the property, I was able to psychically discern that another house had previously stood on the spot and that a murder had occurred in that old house. A review of old records showed that this was, indeed, the case.

The experience of déjà vu, in which you feel as if you have experienced something before, may be an experience of retrocognition. Retrocognition may also be a result of a *reincarnation* experience—your soul may have been in another body, and you are somehow accessing the knowledge from that life experience in this one. As with all other psychic manifestations, you may perceive retrocognitive information via any of the psychic senses.

PSYCHOKINESIS

Psychokinesis, sometimes abbreviated as *PK* and also known as *telekinesis*, is the ability to manipulate objects with your mind. It's a psychic form of "mind over matter."

There are a number of documented cases of psychokinesis, involving people deliberately affecting matter with their minds as well as people doing it unconsciously. Parapsychologists have long recognized that often, a case suspected to involve a *poltergeist* (noisy ghost) is not actually caused by a ghost but rather by a human PK agent who doesn't realize they're affecting matter with their brain's energy. This is called *recurrent spontaneous psychokinesis*, or *RSP*.

Often, these incidents are attributed to teenagers, but anyone who is experiencing a spiritually or emotionally tumultuous period may become the source of poltergeist activity and demonstrate RSP by causing objects to move seemingly on their own. These incidents, which can be frightening and violent, often occur when someone who is struggling with emotional issues or going through a time of upheaval has no outlet for these energies. The brain, struggling to cope, releases energetic signals that cause objects to move. It's sort of a psychic pressure-release valve, and typically the agent is unaware they are causing these disturbing incidents.

Some people are able to consciously and deliberately demonstrate telekinetic powers as well. You've likely seen people with this ability do things such as bend spoons with their minds, levitate objects, or move items in other ways.

In haunted locations when it appears a spirit is moving an object, leaving a voice imprint on a recording medium (called *electronic voice phenomena*, or *EVP*), turning lights on and off, or showing up as a solid image in a photograph or video, parapsychologists have determined this is a form of telekinesis caused by the spiritual energy of the ghost.

Some ways psychokinesis may manifest include:

- Spontaneous combustion of objects (*pyrokinesis*)

- Levitation

- Materializing objects seemingly out of thin air (*apports*)

- Making objects disappear (*deports*)

- Small-scale atmospheric changes, such as dropping the temperature in a room

- Causing percussive noises, such as raps or knocks

- Causing objects to move or stop moving, such as doors opening and closing on their own

- Projecting vocalizations (disembodied voices)

- Imprinting sounds or voices on recording mediums

- Causing disturbances in electricity, such as making lights go on and off or turning on the television or radio with one's mind

- Influencing a random number generator

MEDICAL INTUITION

Medical intuition is having a psychic understanding of something going on physiologically in the human body. This includes recognizing energetic causes for disease as well as simply noticing that disease exists in a physical organism. It is a helpful psychic manifestation for people who work as energy healers, as they are better able to help their healing partners if they understand where disease exists and what its root causes are.

I am medically intuitive, which may be one of the reasons I was so attuned to Jim's coronary artery disease even when he was in denial. Most of my medical intuition comes to me via empathy and clairtangency, but occasionally it also arises via clairsentience or claircognizance. In other words, I feel it in my body and emotions, and sometimes I know something is "off" with someone's health and what that is.

I know a chiropractor who received his medical intuition via clairvoyance. Whenever he had a patient on his table, he was able to see black cones projecting from the places where the patient was experiencing spinal misalignment. I know another energy healer who always hears the information. As she's working on a healing partner, she'll hear something such as "left knee" and know that is where she needs to work next.

Being medically intuitive is a powerful gift, but it's important that someone with this ability not misuse it or run afoul of the law. Unless you have certain medical licenses, you cannot diagnose—doing so is practicing medicine without a license, which is a legal no-no. Therefore, you can use the information in your work with a healing partner, but you can't tell the healing partner they have any specific injury or illness, nor can you contradict or act against a doctor's orders. If you have this ability, I recommend taking a course in working with medical intuition or energy healing (or working with a mentor) so you can learn the best ways to use your gifts and communicate with your healing partners in ways that protect their health and well-being while still protecting you legally. It can be a fine line to walk.

ENERGY HEALING

Energy healing takes many forms, from hands-on modalities such as *Reiki*, *polarity therapy*, and *healing touch* to other forms of vibrational work, such as crystals and sound healing.

While you don't have to have psychic abilities to work as an energy healer, working with your psychic abilities can enhance the process. I rely a great deal on psychic information when I work with my energy healing partners, and I find that most of my students also have intuitive gifts.

The most common gifts I find among energy healers are empathy and clairtangency. I believe empaths are drawn to energy healing work because they are so attuned to how others feel and want to make the world feel better. Energy healing allows them to do this.

I've also found that as people begin to work with energy healing modalities, their psychic gifts become stronger, and without even realizing it, they begin to rely on intuitive information as they work with their healing partners. For example, when I do a sound healing, I never have a set plan. Rather, I rely on my intuition to tell me which bowls, gongs, and chimes to strike, how long to allow them to ring, and so on. Likewise, in crystal healing sessions, I use my abilities to discern what will work best for my healing partners. It's hard to describe, but I will notice a certain resonance between my healing partner and a given crystal that confirms I am using the right crystals for that specific person's needs.

AURA READING

Aura readers can visualize what someone's or something's aura looks like. The *aura* is part of the energy field of every living being and inanimate object. It's created by the object's vibrational frequency, and it surrounds the object in multiple layers of color.

One of my coworkers is an aura reader. She tells me she sees various layers of color surrounding people, animals, plants, and things. It's something she's always been able to do, although anyone can learn to do it with time and patience. One method that may work for you is to hold your hand in front of a white piece of paper and unfocus your eyes as you look at it.

Symbolism of aura colors include the following, which can be either positive or negative expressions. In the case of people, the colors indicate what issues an individual may be working with in their life at the moment:

RED Safety, security, anger, passion, sexual energy

BLACK Boundaries, protection, darkness (evil), soul damage

ORANGE Belonging, courage, ignorance, creative ideation

BROWN Environmentalism, muddled emotions, dogma, connection to nature

YELLOW Self-esteem, willpower, sociability, responsibility

GOLD Wealth, prosperity

GREEN Love, jealousy, guilt

PINK Compassion, femininity, maturity

BLUE Communication, speaking and living one's truth, judgment, criticism, creative expression

TURQUOISE Spirituality, physical or emotional healing

PURPLE/VIOLET Connection of mental and spiritual energy, critical thinking, mental acuity, psychic ability

WHITE Purity, spiritual evolution, newness, innocence

The ability to see auras allows you to understand things about the energy of the person, animal, plant, or object you are looking at. The colors each have specific meanings that can provide insight into the emotional, physical, mental, and spiritual energy of whoever or whatever you're reading.

PSYCHOMETRY

Psychometry is the ability to receive spiritual information through touch—someone with psychometric ability can touch an object and glean information by doing so. For instance, my grandmother had to touch Christmas presents to know what was in them. As another example, when I play my antique piano, images flash through my mind of where the piano has been and other people who have played it. It only happens when I'm touching the piano.

When you touch an object, you may receive psychic information via any of the clairs, and it may be specific or general. It's great as party entertainment, and if you cultivate this ability, you can also use it to assess the energy of objects (particularly antiques or secondhand objects) that you bring into your home. I love to go to antique stores to practice this ability, because by touching the objects in the store, I can gain insight into other periods in history. I seldom bring antiques home, however, because objects brought into a space can affect the energy of that space, and I'm careful about the energy I surround myself with. I've learned in my work with some of my clients just how often bringing an antique or other secondhand object into one's home can affect its energy.

I recommend that before you bring any object home, you touch it, close your eyes, and see how it makes you feel. If something feels off when you touch it, don't bring it home. Trust your intuition and the information you receive.

People can also use psychometry to select items for personal growth and energy healing, such as crystals or singing bowls. In chapter 6, I'll offer a few different methods for developing and testing psychometry that will help you to choose items to support your growth.

ASTRAL TRAVEL

Astral travel is the ability for your spirit to leave your body and explore other places on Earth or in other dimensions, whether in dreams, meditation, or a waking state. Many people have their first astral travel experience, also known as an *out-of-body experience* (*OBE*), in a dream state. For example, two of my friends had the same "dream" on the same night in which they met up and had a conversation. It was only the next day as they chatted about it that they realized their dream experiences had been exactly the same. This was most likely a case of spontaneous astral travel through dreams.

Other people may have this experience in a waking or meditative state, or sometimes during a *near-death experience* (*NDE*). For instance, people who have undergone cardiac arrest and been resuscitated often report hovering above their bodies and observing medical personnel working to save their lives. These clinically dead people are able to verify conversations and actions they experienced. This is a form of astral travel, although the person traveling doesn't venture far from their body.

Initially, astral travel may occur spontaneously. However, with time, if you wish to deliberately induce it, you can learn to do so using something called the "roll out" technique. It's best to try this as you're drifting off to sleep or slipping into deep meditation when you're in the twilight state where you're still somewhat aware but drifting toward dreams.

When you recognize that you're in that state, visualize yourself rolling sideways out of your body and moving around the room. Start small. As you become more adept, you can try to travel further.

CHANNELING

Channeling involves stepping aside and allowing the energy of another entity to communicate through you. It's one of the most misunderstood manifestations of psychic ability. It is not possession; many people believe that in order to channel, you must completely abandon your body and let another entity take over, but that's not necessarily the case, although that is how it works for some channels. Instead, it is a willingness to set aside ego and personal agendas and allow the information to flow through you.

In a way, channeling is a form of reporting. I channel a group of entities who have identified themselves to me as the George Collective (I call them the Georges for short). They've been with me since I was a child, and their information and the way they communicate through me has evolved. At first, the information I received from them was mostly simple, childish poems, pictures, and stories, but over the years it has progressed to complex works that often contain thoughts or ideas that thoroughly surprise me and contain far more universal wisdom than I possess. I believe most of my books are at least partially channeled. Additionally, starting in January 2020, the Georges began dictating specific information that they wanted me to share with people, much of it messages of hope about the opportunities for humanity arising from the world events that began in early 2020 and continued throughout the year as other major world events happened. My experience with that has been similar to that of the Dictaphone I used to type reports from a former boss.

One way to begin channeling is to sit down with a piece of paper (or your computer) and ask questions. Then, write or type the first information that comes to your mind without judgment or censorship. This is a simple form of channeling.

A number of public figures have served as channels, including Neale Donald Walsch in the Conversations with God series, Lee Carroll in the Kryon channelings, Jane Roberts in the Seth channelings, Pat Rodegast in the Emmanuel channelings, and Esther Hicks in the Abraham-Hicks channelings. One of the most popular spiritual manuals of modern times, *A Course in Miracles* is channeled, and some believe many, if not all, spiritual texts such as the Bible and the Koran have been channeled.

Channeling is simply a way to bring deep spiritual wisdom from a higher source to embodied humans. The people who channel are willing to set aside their own personal egos and desires to share the information in the purest form they receive it.

ANIMAL COMMUNICATION

Animal communication is the ability to psychically communicate with animals. My friend Karen is an animal communicator who has an affinity for all animals. She can also use her psychic perceptions for humans, but because her heart lies with animals, this is how she chooses to manifest her abilities.

Animal communicators (also called *pet psychics*) may communicate with living pets or animals that have died to help humans understand their needs or provide comfort.

My Brussels griffon, Monkey, has benefited from Karen's animal communication abilities, and as a result her humans also sleep better at night. Monkey is incredibly spoiled, and while I tell her she's not the boss of me, she clearly is. For a period of about seven years, when Monkey got out of bed in the middle of the night, instead of coming back to bed under her own power, she would bark and wait for someone to come get her. You could not outwait her. If we ignored her, she'd continue to do it until someone got up. Sometimes, this happened multiple times a night.

Finally, in desperation (and exhaustion), I reached out to Karen. She had a telepathic conversation with Monkey and told me that every night before I went to bed, I should tell her, "I'm going to bed now. If you get up, I expect you to come back to bed on your own without waking me."

I was skeptical, but I did what Karen said. Within two nights, the behavior stopped. Now, occasionally I forget to tell Monkey that before I go to bed. On those nights, she almost always tries to revert to the way things were; she'll get up and bark until I yell, "*Go to bed!*" Then, she'll hustle her little heinie to bed, and all will be well.

Karen also helped me when my fifteen-year-old toy fox terrier, Spike, neared the end of his life. About a week before he died, Spike, whose trachea was collapsing, began fainting if he did anything too strenuous. It was sad to see, and I reached out to Karen to find out whether he wanted to continue as he was or be euthanized. Karen told me that Spike wanted to have as much time with us as possible and that we should do the best we could to make him comfortable. She said when he was ready to go, he'd let us know.

For the next week, I did what Karen said. I kept him comfortable and gave him a lot of love and Reiki. I spent most of my time with him because I knew he was nearing the end. Over a three-day weekend, Spike stopped breathing for several minutes as I sat holding him. I told Jim, "Spike has died," and Jim ran over crying. As Jim reached him, Spike, who hadn't breathed for several minutes, twitched and heaved in a huge breath. I knew it was time to make an appointment to euthanize him and scheduled his appointment for the Tuesday after the long weekend.

Tuesday morning at about 2:00 a.m., I woke knowing that it was time and that Spike wouldn't make it to his vet appointment. I got up and carried him into the living room. For a few minutes, he wandered around the house sniffing and looking at things, as if he was getting one last impression of his life with us. Then, I took him over to the couch, sat down, and channeled Reiki to him. He died peacefully with me holding him.

I was able to sense Spike was ready to die because he had been my dog for fifteen years, and I was very close to him. I'm not someone who normally communicates with animals psychically, but in that moment because of our close bond, I was able to.

If you feel connected to animals, this may be a psychic ability you already possess or can cultivate. Animal communication provides deeper insight into the creatures that share our planet and our lives.

GEOSENSITIVITY

Geosensitivity is the ability to sense shifts or changes in the planet Earth. For me, this manifests as the ability to sense an earthquake before it happens. For Jim, it's his uncanny knack for navigating without a map anywhere he goes. For others, it may be the ability to sense and predict other planetary, environmental, or atmospheric events, such as storms, volcanic eruptions, or tidal waves. As with all manifestations of psychic ability, if you are geosensitive, you may be able perceive this information through any of the clairs.

People who are geosensitive often are environmentally aware and have an affinity for nature. This may manifest as environmental activism, interest in things such as storm chasing or geology, or a love of outdoor adventures such as mountain climbing or surfing.

For example, both Jim and I love the mountains and the sea, and we spend as much time outdoors as we can. I'm happiest when I am either in the water or in the mountains; I feel like the earth speaks to me the most clearly when I am there.

* *

There are other, less common ways psychic abilities can manifest and be engaged. For example, police psychics work with the police force to provide insight into crimes, missing persons reports, and more. All of these manifestations of the ability don't exist for personal material gain, but rather to support the highest and greatest good of all involved.

PART II

Developing & Managing Psychic Ability

CHAPTER 4

Psychic Protection

· ·

It is essential when you work with psychic ability that you learn how to manage it and protect yourself energetically. In the introduction, I mentioned that before I understood my psychic abilities, I experienced a great deal of anxiety—something I suspected was an undiagnosed generalized anxiety disorder and/or social anxiety. Since I started working with my abilities and have learned to manage them and protect myself, however, those anxieties have disappeared from my life completely. It's not unusual for people with strong psychic abilities to experience what they think are mental health issues such as anxiety, depression, or other emotional disorders until they learn to work with their abilities and protect themselves from free-floating psychic energy.

Likewise, I have a number of friends who are now working psychics. As we've talked about our times before psychic (BP) and after psychic (AP), we've discovered that all of us had issues such as anxiety and mood swings during the BP era that cleared up once we entered our AP period and gained insight about controlling our abilities and using the psychic protection techniques outlined in this chapter.

CLAIMING YOUR POWER AS A PSYCHIC

If you plan to work with your psychic abilities, it's essential that you also learn how to manage and control them. The first and most important step is to acknowledge and accept them.

Psychic abilities are a gift that should enhance your life, not diminish it. They exist to serve your highest good. Therefore, before you begin to work with your gifts, you must first come to terms with and be willing to accept them as a natural part of your life. If you skip this step and continue to feel embarrassed by, doubtful of, or hesitant about your abilities, then you will remain at the mercy of your gifts instead of being able to work with them to serve your greatest good.

I believe the reason so many people with psychic abilities struggle emotionally, mentally, spiritually, and even physically is because we live in a society that says these perfectly natural abilities are either unnatural or not real. It's challenging to not feel comfortable living your truth, to not understand or be able to control your gifts, to feel you must deny your natural abilities, and to try to fit within a social structure that is unsupportive of who you are at your core.

I spent many years struggling to come to terms with my abilities. This was partially because I was raised in a social and religious structure that viewed psychic abilities as being misguided at best and fraudulent, deluded, or evil at worst. This is an uncomfortable position to be in that drives many with strong psychic abilities underground or causes them to deny and ignore their Source-given gifts altogether.

I can't tell you how to come to terms with your own abilities or how to live in a society that doesn't support them; that is an individual journey that helps each of us to grow as souls. However, I can offer insights about some of the ways I and other psychics I know have found our way forward into empowerment.

Consider Who You Are Trying to Please

Examine why it matters to you what other people think. It took my dad dying for me to realize how much time I spent seeking others' approval and what a waste of time, energy, effort, and emotion that was. I kept my abilities hidden from myself and others for many years and denied myself my truth while denying others the opportunity to know the true me and to benefit from my gifts. What I ultimately came to realize is that I have no control over what others think about me, and by not being who I truly was, I was attempting to control their impressions of me. This is always a losing game.

Now I understand that if someone doesn't like me or want to be around me because of my abilities, that's their issue. It's exhausting to always try to be what everyone wants you to be and freeing to finally step into and embody your truth. If this is your journey, know that you are not alone and that you have the love and support of many in the psychic community who have walked a similar path and emerged into the freedom that exists on the other side.

Cultivate Support

Another thing many psychics have found helpful as they begin to live their truth is finding a community of like-minded individuals who understand and share your abilities. There are many different communities that accept people who have decided to step into their power as psychics, including energy healing groups, spiritual centers, paranormal communities, and psychic communities.

You may also want to consider talk therapy or life coaching with a supportive and empathic adviser to help you as you claim your power as a psychic. I know many psychics who have degrees in psychology and provide therapy services that are nonjudgmental and accepting of people coming to terms with their abilities.

Educate Yourself

Whether you find a mentor, take classes, read books like this one, or attend conferences, learning more about your gifts will help you to recognize them, understand how normal they actually are, and begin to use them in ways that serve your greatest good.

Help Someone Else

Since psychic gifts exist to help humans, once you begin to feel confident in your abilities, the best thing you can do for your own mental, emotional, and spiritual health is to use those gifts in ways that serve humanity. This is a source of joy and empowerment for many psychics, including me.

CONNECTING WITH SPIRIT GUIDES

All souls who are embodied have spirit guides—helpful spirits on the other side that provide us with guidance as we navigate life as an incarnated soul (see page 168). Some people have close and intimate relationships with their spirit guides, while others may only notice their guidance in cryptic or brief flashes of insight, such as a premonition not to take a certain street to work or a dream that suggests they go get their thyroid checked.

Regardless of whether you know your spirit guides or not, however, they are always there, working for you and trying to provide guidance in the ways you are most likely to perceive it. I believe they are the source of psychic abilities. Your spirit guides are always with you, and they have your back. It is their fondest wish that you connect with them and learn to hear and accept their guidance.

If you have yet to connect with your spirit guides, it's high time you did. Connecting with your guides can strengthen your abilities and give you better control over them. One of the easiest ways to connect with your guides is to acknowledge their existence, express gratitude for their guidance until now, and ask them for communication. Many people start working with their spirit guides by asking for specific signs. For example, you could say "If this is the right thing for me, please show me a white feather." Then, keep your eyes open for a white feather. As you begin to tune in to their signs, you will become more aware of other signs and guidance as well.

You can also ask your spirit guides to come to you in meditation or dreams. Then, practice awareness and be open to how they may approach you. Using the divination techniques in chapter 6 also provides an excellent way to communicate with your guides.

Spirit guides will use any method they can to connect with you. They may send signs, use numerology (see page 104), talk to you in dreams and visions (page 106), send a helpful stranger to speak with you, put the right song on the radio at the moment you need to hear it, and more. Sometimes they speak in the language of symbols, and sometimes they are far less subtle.

One of my more profound experiences with my spirit guides happened when I was concerned about my husband's heart problems. Just before he finally admitted to having chest pains, I started finding tiny red foil hearts in weird places in my house, such as on the kitchen counter, on a couch where I was sitting, and on my pillow. In all, I received seven of these red hearts, and they stopped appearing the day my husband had his angioplasty. In total over his three heart surgeries, he has had seven stents placed. I don't believe it was a coincidence that my guides left hearts to symbolize his heart problem or that their number was the same as the number of stents he has had placed.

PSYCHIC SHIELDING

Another thing you'll want to learn to do as soon as possible is to put up a psychic shield. This gives you great control over your abilities and allows you to control when you receive psychic information. It can also block out negative energy and excessive psychic "noise" from others so you are safe and protected as you go about your business.

I sometimes use affirmations or statements of intention—for some people, this might be prayer or spell work—as a method of psychic shielding. To do this, I make a positive statement, such as "I am grateful I receive information that serves the greatest good, and I am protected from any negative energy as I go about my work." I speak this affirmation either aloud or in my mind daily, typically first thing in the morning, before I do psychic work, and before I go to sleep at night. Notice it is stated as a positive (as opposed to "I don't receive information from dark sources, and I don't receive negative energy"), and it expresses gratitude for the protection it provides. Feel free to use my affirmation or come up with your own.

I also use visualization to create a psychic shield that blocks out any psychic information. This is so that if I'm someplace where I don't have the bandwidth to receive psychic information, or if I'm in a situation that feels like it might be psychically harmful, I can block any outside energy completely. It's a simple visualization, and it's easy to personalize for your own needs. To put up a psychic shield, close your eyes and take a few deep breaths, breathing in through your nose and out through your mouth. When you feel you are in a calm and focused state, visualize a shield popping out from your solar plexus (around your diaphragm) and surrounding you completely.

Your shield can be made of any material; mine is a clear bubble, so I can see out but nothing else can enter. Some people make theirs a suit of armor, a brick wall, or even a blanket. I find that most people won't know what their shield is made of until they try visualizing it. Make sure you push the shield out from inside of you instead of building it around you. In this way, it will push away any energy instead of trapping it inside of your shield with you.

I recommend resetting your shield every few hours when you first start. As you gain more control of your abilities, you may choose to set it only at the start of a day or when you don't wish to be disturbed.

Filters

Once you've learned to apply your shield and keep it in place, you can add filters to allow only the energy and information you want to reach you. Doing so is simply a statement of intention: for example, "I will allow information that serves my greatest good to come into my shield" or "I will allow my spirit guides to communicate through my shield."

You can filter for any type of energy, and either one type or multiple types of energy at a time. The goal ultimately is to block the psychic signals that serve as a distraction while allowing in those that are beneficial.

You may not always want to allow a filter. Sometimes, you just need to be in your own space with your own thoughts. In that case, reapply your original shield and enjoy your me time.

GROUNDING

Grounding is an essential tool for any psychic. Many people working with their psychic abilities tend to not be terribly grounded; for the first forty years of my life, I felt as if I didn't live in my body and instead drifted somewhere just above it. Until I learned to ground, I was unable to figure out how to be present in my body, which negatively impacted my physical health.

Learning to properly ground can help you to be more focused and centered. It protects your mental, physical, and spiritual health. It can also keep you from experiencing the spaced-out, light-headed feelings people new to working with their psychic abilities often notice. It's a way of caring for your body and mind while your spirit seeks information from higher sources, and it's an essential tool for every psychic.

One of the easiest ways to ground is to go barefoot and keep your feet flat on the floor. People who have taken my in-person classes or had a healing or reading with me know that when I perform these tasks, I am always barefoot. In one class that I was teaching in a new venue, I initially tried to wear shoes. When I finally decided to take them off, one of the students, who had taken a few of my classes, told me that she had been waiting and wondering when I would. I spend most of my indoor time barefoot, and I go barefoot outdoors as much as the weather allows.

If it's not possible to be barefoot all the time, you can also use a simple visualization to ground yourself. Just keep your feet flat on the floor and your eyes closed, then visualize roots growing from the bottoms of your feet and extending deep into the earth. You can perform this exercise standing up or even sitting on the floor. If you do it while you're sitting on the floor, visualize the roots growing from your root chakra (at the base of your tailbone) instead of from your feet.

PSYCHIC PROTECTION TOOLS

Another great way for psychics to protect themselves is by using various psychic protection tools, such as crystals, prayers and affirmations, visualization, and herbs.

Crystals

Black and red crystals, such as black tourmaline, obsidian, shungite, hematite, garnet, and ruby, all serve as excellent sources of psychic protection. They also facilitate grounding, which is a nice side effect. I recommend wearing a ring containing one of these stones on the pinky of your nondominant hand, which is the finger that represents personal boundaries. This helps to set a boundary of energetic protection. If the crystal or ring breaks, it means it has absorbed as much negative energy as it can. Return it to the earth by burying it and then replace it.

I also recommend either wearing or carrying in a pocket a smoky quartz crystal. Smoky quartz transmutes negative energy to positive, so it's excellent for psychic protection. I have surrounded my entire property and my house with smoky quartz crystals so that any energy that enters my personal space is positive.

Prayers of Protection, Visualization, and Affirmation

You can use any of these tools alone, together, or in concert with other protection techniques. I tend to prefer affirmations. For example, when I get in my car, I always use the affirmation "Spirit, go before me and make my way easy, safe, and passable." In my psychic work, I typically affirm something such as "I give thanks for the receipt of beneficial information that serves the greatest good of my client" or "Thank you to my spirit guides for protecting and guiding me as I work with my client."

Find a prayer, visualization, or affirmation that feels right for you and suits the situation you're in. A simple statement of intention is all you really need to protect yourself psychically. For a visualization, you can picture white light pouring into your space and into your body, filling it and washing away any negativity.

Herbs

Many psychics also like to work with the smoke of burning herbs, often sage or palo santo, to provide protection and create an energetic space for their psychic work. If you burn sage, know that it clears away any energy in a space, leaving sort of an energetic vacuum. Therefore, you'll want to follow it up with another burning herb to bring in positive energy, such as sweetgrass, lavender, cedar, or palo santo.

I'm a huge fan of palo santo; I prefer it to sage because it both clears away negative energy and invites in positive energy. I burn it before every class and session I hold, and I also burn it and fan the smoke all around my home after anything negative has occurred, such as an illness or an argument. I also cleanse my home with palo santo smoke every week on Sunday morning to help maintain the positive vibes. You can use incense in much the same manner.

Sound

You can also use sound for psychic protection, whether you strike a singing bowl to clear out any negative energy or use a mantra or protective chant, such as "I am safe and protected" or "Aad guray nameh" which is a yoga mantra of white light protection. Repeat the mantra aloud 108 times using a set of *mala* beads or prayer beads to count your recitation.

· ·

All of the techniques described in this chapter are essential tools in your psychic arsenal. It is important you learn to control your psychic ability and protect yourself energetically, both for your own well-being and for the well-being of those you are helping. Once you have mastered these techniques, you can begin to play with tools that may help focus your psychic perception.

CHAPTER 5

Using Psychic Tools

· ·

There are many tools to help focus psychic energy when you wish to tune in to your abilities. These can boost your confidence as a psychic as well as provide structure and direction when you're seeking intuitive guidance.

For example, I provide psychic readings for clients, and I frequently use a tarot or oracle deck. It serves as a point of focus and provides confirmation for the psychic information I receive. I find I don't need these tools, but having them available helps me to feel more confident when I do readings.

I'll let you in on a secret: every time I perform a psychic reading, I'm certain I'm going to blow it. I realize this is my ego talking, but it still happens every time. While I've grown confident in my abilities, I still fear I'm going to freeze up when I'm face-to-face with someone who wants a reading. It has yet to happen, but I always have my tarot or oracle deck handy just in case.

Over the years, I've discovered how it typically works for me—I receive information and pull a card, and the card provides the same information I receive psychically. Since I tend to be all over the place during readings as I'm bombarded by psychic sensory information, the cards help me to focus on the information that's important for my client to receive. The tools also help me to make better sense of symbolic psychic information.

While you don't need to work with tools when you're accessing psychic information, using them can boost confidence, help you focus, and confirm the information you receive. Fortunately, there are plenty of tools you can use. Find some that resonate with you and try them.

DIVINATION TOOLS

Divination is the practice of seeking information about future events or the unknown through psychic means. More practically, it involves using tools to seek answers through psychic channels, from spirit guides, or from the collective consciousness. For example, when someone uses dowsing rods to locate water, it's a form of divination.

There are hundreds of divination methods, many of them specific to various cultures. Many divination terms end in the suffix -mancy, which means "divination by the means of." So, if you encounter a word that ends in this suffix, chances are it is a form of divination.

Because there are hundreds of methods of divination, I can't cover all of them, so I've chosen some that I find the most useful for people working with their psychic gifts.

Pendulums

Divination using a pendulum is also called *pallomancy*. Many psychics enjoy working with pendulums because they are plentiful, affordable, and easy to use. Pendulums may be made from gemstones, glass, metal, and many other materials. The line holding the pendulum is typically a string or a metal chain. You can even make your own simple pendulum by tying a ring to a string (a common form of divination that women have historically used to determine the gender of a baby).

Choose a pendulum you feel drawn to. When considering one, hold it in your nondominant hand and see whether you notice resonance, or a feeling of "rightness" or connection. If you don't, keep looking. If you do, it's probably the pendulum for you. You'll find pendulums in crystal and metaphysical shops, in spiritual bookstores, and at metaphysical fairs. Don't rush your selection process; it's essential you resonate with your pendulum so you can work with it effectively.

When you bring your pendulum home, cleanse it right away with palo santo or sage smoke or by placing it in a vessel with a selenite crystal for a few hours. Cleanse it in the same manner between uses to maintain its frequency. I keep mine in a selenite bowl so it is always freshly cleansed when I'm ready to use it.

After cleansing your pendulum for the first time and before you begin to work with it, carry it with you in a pocket or in your hand for a day or two so your energy can meld with its energy. This "getting to know you" process is an important step in being ready to work with your pendulum. I recently acquired a new pendulum that I was drawn to

Pendulums might move in the following ways:

- Swinging in a straight line toward and away from you

- Swinging in a straight line from side to side

- Swinging in a straight line diagonally

- Swinging in a clockwise or counterclockwise circle

- Spinning clockwise or counterclockwise

- No movement

on a visit to Mount Shasta in California, and I even slept with it under my pillow for a few nights before I started to work with it.

The easiest way to work with a pendulum is to hold it and ask yes or no questions. The way the pendulum swings provides an answer to your question.

Each pendulum responds differently. There's no set way to interpret what movement means, so you need to ask your pendulum. Once your pendulum tells you what each movement represents, it will always answer your questions using the same motion.

To establish what your pendulum's movements mean, do the following:

1. Sit at a table with your feet flat on the floor. Place one elbow on the table with your forearm extended perpendicular to it.

2. Drape the chain or string of the pendulum over the edge of your pointer finger with the pendulum dangling and lightly hold the chain in place with your thumb. Holding it this way keeps you from subconsciously moving the pendulum with imperceptible muscle movements, something known as the *ideomotor effect*. Alternatively, suspend your pendulum from a hook so there's no chance at all you'll influence its movement.

3. Take a few deep breaths and make the following requests, pausing and allowing the pendulum to move before you ask the next.

   - Show me yes

   - Show me no

   - Show me maybe

   - Show me a nonresponse, or it's not for me to know

   Record how your pendulum responds to each query so you have it for future reference. For example, my pendulum moves in a clockwise circle for yes, swings back and forth for no, swings diagonally left top right bottom for maybe, and doesn't move (or stops moving) when there's no response or it's not for me to know.

4. Finish your session by expressing gratitude and cleanse your pendulum.

Moving forward, when you work with your pendulum, do the following:

1. Sit at the table holding the cleansed pendulum as indicated on page 91.

2. Close your eyes, take a few deep breaths, and make an opening affirmation or prayer. For example, "I give thanks to my higher self and my guides for communicating with me through this pendulum and for providing the information that serves the highest and greatest good."

3. Now you can ask yes or no questions, leaving plenty of time for the pendulum to react.

4. When you're done, express gratitude and cleanse your pendulum.

Palm Reading

Palm reading, also called *palmistry*, is a form of divination in which a trained reader examines the anatomy of the hand and uses their findings to predict various aspects of someone's personality as well as general information about marriages, life challenges, and more.

My friend Clay is a gifted palm reader who has taught me much about the art and science of palmistry. I've had him read my palm a few times, and it's uncanny how accurate he is. When he reads palms, he looks at features such as:

- How a person holds their hand up when they wave
- Finger lengths
- Lines on the palm
- Features that interrupt those lines, such as islands or small crisscrosses
- Branches from the lines
- Skin texture and color
- Fingerprints

Palmistry is a complex form of divination requiring significant study to master, but once you do, it provides astonishingly accurate information. See the Resources for Psychics section at the end of this book for some palm reading resources to learn more.

Bibliomancy

Bibliomancy (also called *chartomancy*) is a form of divination in which you look to written works to provide information and focus. It's an easy form of divination in that it requires no special supplies except for books. Some people prefer to use specific books, such as religious or spiritual texts, but any book will do as long as it is a physical rather than a digital one. I recommend selecting a book that draws you when you are ready to begin a session; I typically walk to my bookshelf, close my eyes, and grab one. I trust the universe will provide the exact book I need for my bibliomancy session, whether it's a Tom Clancy novel, a hiking directory, or a spiritual text.

To conduct a bibliomancy session:

1. Select a book you are drawn to you or one that you find meaningful.

2. Sit somewhere you won't be disturbed. Place your feet flat on the floor and hold the book in your lap or place it on a table in front of you.

3. Take a few deep breaths and say an opening affirmation or prayer. For example, "I give thanks that the answers I seek are provided in the pages of this book" or "Tell me what I need to know."

4. Close your eyes and ask your question. When you're ready, with your eyes still closed, open the book, allowing it to open to any random page.

5. Keep your eyes closed and use your index finger to point to a spot on the page. Allow your finger to land wherever it lands without trying to control it.

6. Read the passage where your finger landed—that's your answer. Record the answers you receive for later study if you wish.

7. Repeat for additional questions.

8. When you're finished, hold the book in both hands and offer thanks for the information you have received.

Runes

Runecasting is a form of casting objects, such as dice or bones, to receive answers to your queries. This form of divination is called *cleromancy*. Runes are tiles made from various materials that have runic symbols written on them, each with a specific meaning.

You can use runes in various ways, but one of the easiest is to simply ask a question and then choose a rune. Place the runes facedown to draw them. Pick one you feel drawn to or close your eyes and choose one after you ask your question. The rune's meaning will provide your answer.

There are more complex ways to use runes as well, but they require study and practice. See the Resources for Psychics section for more information.

I Ching

The *I Ching* (pronounced "ee ching"), or *Book of Changes*, is an ancient Chinese book of wisdom that has been used for centuries as a form of divination and guidance. I've taken a few classes in reading the *I Ching*, and I consult it frequently both for personal guidance and in my work as a psychic.

Working with the *I Ching* involves a combination of bibliomancy and cleromancy. You'll need:

- Three coins (I use Chinese coins, but any coin with a "heads" and a "tails" side works)
- Pen and paper
- An *I Ching* interpretation book (see the Resources for Psychics section for a few recommendations)

To conduct an *I Ching* session:

1. Go someplace you won't be disturbed. Take a few deep breaths.

2. Ask a question. It could be specific or it could be a general request, such as "Tell me what I need to know."

3. Cast the three coins six times, recording the patterns of heads and tails for each casting.

4. Each cast creates one line of a hexagram, which you will draw from bottom to top as you cast the coins.

Record lines from each cast as follows:

Three tails: a horizontal line broken in the center with an X in the middle

———— X ————

Three heads: an unbroken horizontal line with an X in the middle

———— X ————

Two heads, one tail: a broken horizontal line

————   ————

Two tails, one head: an unbroken horizontal line

————————

So, a completed hexagram might end up looking like this after six casts:

```
————————————————  Cast 6
————————   ————————  Cast 5
————————   ————————  Cast 4
————————   ————————  Cast 3
————————  X  ————————  Cast 2
————————————————  Cast 1
```

5. Once you have your final hexagram, change any line with an X through it to the opposite. So, if you have an X through a solid line, change it to a broken line and vice versa. Like so:

```
————————————————
————————   ————————
————————   ————————
————————   ————————
```

6. The bottom three lines make up your first *trigram*, and the top three lines make up your second trigram. Your *I Ching* interpretation book will have a chart at either the front or the back; locate the bottom trigram in the vertical column and the top trigram in the horizontal row. The intersection of these two trigrams on the chart will provide a number to look up in your interpretation.

7. Turn to that section in the book and read what is there to have your question answered.

Dowsing Rods

Dowsing, or divining, uses L-shaped rods or poles called *dowsing rods*. These may be made of various materials, although copper seems to be the most commonly available for premade rods. When you dowse, you'll need two rods—you'll hold one in each hand. Hold the short part of the rod loosely enough that the rod can spin in your hands. Keep your elbows tucked firmly into your sides, hold your hands and forearms parallel to the floor, and make sure the long edge of the rod is parallel to the floor as well.

Dowsing has been used for centuries to find hidden sources of water, but dowsing rods are also great tools for other forms of divination.

Movements dowsing rods may make include:

- Crossing

- Pointing away from each other

- Pointing toward each other

- Pointing straight ahead

- Pointing toward you

- Parallel, pointing in one direction or another

- Spinning

When I first started working with my dowsing rods, all they would do was spin wildly, which was pretty trippy. However, once I adapted to their energy and they to mine, I was able to use the rods to answer yes or no questions or to point to things.

As with a pendulum (see page 91), you'll need to establish how your rods respond to you the first time you work with them by asking them to show you their yes, no, maybe, and no responses. Then, once you've established how the rods move for specific responses, you can begin to work with them in much the same way you would work with a pendulum.

You can also use dowsing rods to find lost items—something I find extremely valuable since I lose stuff all the time, particularly my car keys. To do this:

1. Hold the dowsing rods as described above.

2. Say aloud, "I am looking for _____. Please help me find it. Point in the direction where I should walk, and spin when I should stop or switch directions."

3. Wait for the rods to point parallel in a direction and begin to walk that way. When the rods spin, stop and ask the same thing again. Doing this, the rods will lead you to the location of your lost item.

Other Divination Tools

These are just a few of my favorite divination tools, but there are hundreds more. Some other forms of divination you can learn about and try include:

• Reading tea leaves or coffee grounds (*tasseomancy*)

• Divining with a compass or needles (*acutomancy*)

• Face reading (*physiognomy*)

• Reading bumps on skin (*bumpology*)

• Smoke reading (*capnomancy*)

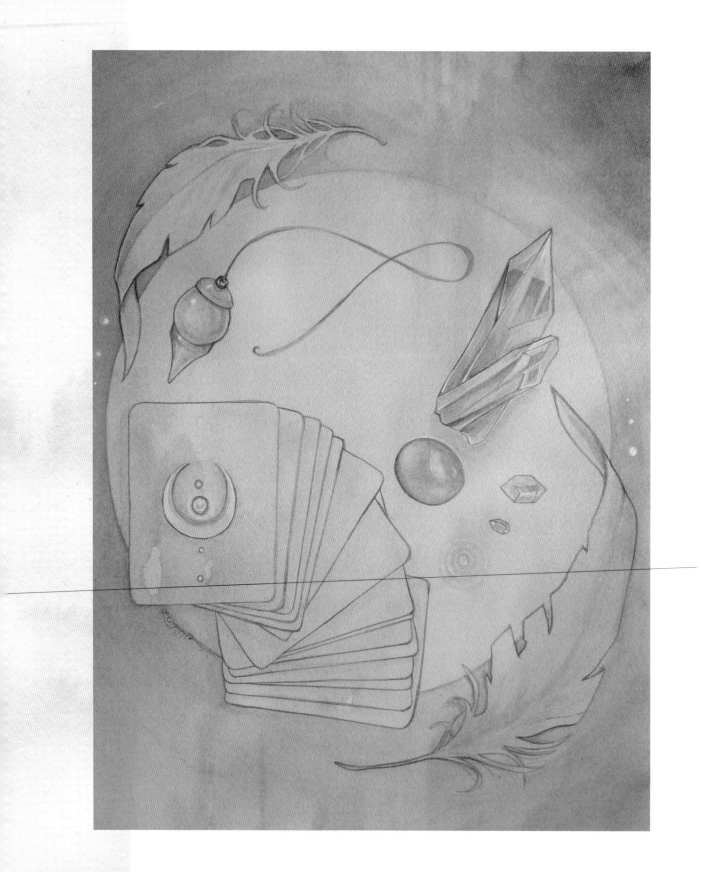

TAROT AND ORACLE CARDS

Tarot and oracle cards are my go-to psychic tools. The modern classic tarot deck is the Rider-Waite or Rider-Waite-Smith deck. It contains twenty-two Major Arcana cards, which symbolize the main archetypes in the journey of the human soul, and four suits of fourteen Minor Arcana cards each. The suits correspond with the four classical elements: Earth (Coins/Pentacles), Air (Swords), Water (Cups), and Fire (Wands). The fourteen cards in each suit are ace through ten, Page, Knight, Queen, and King.

Learning to read tarot and understand its symbolism requires some study in order to quickly interpret the cards as you draw them—you'll find a few great books that teach you how to do this in the Resources for Psychics section. However, there's another way to interpret them that doesn't require any study: simply look at the images and see what they bring to mind.

There are numerous different tarot decks available, many with fun designs, different themes, and interesting symbolism. Each generally comes with a booklet to assist you in interpreting the cards as you draw them, which is helpful as you learn. One of my favorite tarot decks aside from the Rider-Waite-Smith classic deck is the Osho Zen Tarot, which has beautiful illustrations.

Oracle cards aren't based on tarot; instead, each offers its own system of reading. These also typically come with their own booklets to help you interpret them, or you can rely on the images on the cards as a guide.

You can learn classic tarot spreads or try these simple techniques that don't require specialized study or understanding:

- Ask a question and draw a single card to answer it

- Ask a question and do a past-present-future spread by drawing three cards and placing them next to one another, with the left card representing the past, the center card representing the present, and the right card representing the future

SCRYING

Scrying involves gazing at something—often a reflective surface—in order to receive psychic information. The best-known form of scrying uses a crystal ball, although there are many other methods.

The trick with scrying is to clear your mind, unfocus your eyes, and gaze at the surface, allowing images to come to you. It's pretty wild, but it's also a super powerful way for even non-"visual" people to experience clairvoyant visions. It typically works best for seeking specific information, so you may want to state an intention or question before you try, but you can also try it to receive general information by saying, "Tell me what I need to know."

Start a scrying session by taking several calming breaths. It helps to minimize other sensory stimuli by going somewhere you won't be disturbed, playing white noise, and darkening the room except for a task light focused on your scrying object.

Be patient. As with other techniques, the more you practice, the more proficient you'll become. Release your expectations and allow any information that arises to come to you. If you start to feel stressed, end your session and try again another time.

Some objects you can gaze at to scry include:

- A crystal ball or glass ball, or crystals in other forms
- A mirror
- Water in a bowl, sink, or pool
- A candle flame or fire
- Clouds or the sky
- Smoke or fog
- A TV screen with a static pattern
- A white piece of paper with a light shining behind it

AUTOMATIC WRITING AND DRAWING

Automatic writing or drawing is another of my favorite ways to connect with Spirit. As with other tools, learning to use it takes patience, and the more you practice, the easier it gets.

Many people think automatic writing and drawing occurs when spirits move your writing implement (or fingers, if you're typing) for you. Sometimes it happens that way, but not always. I've probably experienced four or five instances of automatic writing throughout my life in which I was sitting and doodling one minute, and when I looked down, time had passed and I noticed I'd written or drawn something significant. But that's typically the exception instead of the rule.

The rest of the time, I work at automatic writing; it's like taking dictation from the universe and is very similar to (if not the same thing as) channeling. Here's a simple process for automatic writing:

1. Go someplace you won't be disturbed. Sit comfortably with your feet flat on the floor.

2. Take a few deep breaths.

3. When you are feeling calm, relaxed, and connected, ask a question and put pen to paper.

4. Begin writing (or drawing) the first thing that comes to mind without judging or censoring.

5. If you feel "stuck," continue writing the same word over and over (or going over the last line you drew) until you unstick.

6. Continue until your question is answered.

7. Express your gratitude for the answer.

In the beginning, start with short sessions of ten minutes or so. You can increase these with time. Be patient and allow the information to flow.

OUIJA AND OTHER TALKING BOARDS

Talking boards are highly controversial in some circles because of an unfounded worry they may connect to something demonic. However, they are simply another tool to connect to psychic information.

In the modern era, the belief that Ouija boards are evil and create a risk of demonic possession was likely revived by the movie *The Exorcist*, in which twelve-year-old Regan is possessed by a demon after talking to an entity called Captain Howdy on her Ouija board. I've never had a dark or negative experience with a talking board—though I do recommend that when working with a board, as with any other psychic tool, you use a method of psychic protection as discussed in chapter 4.

There are a few concerns with using the Ouija board, however, that have nothing to do with demonic possession or negative energy but rather with unduly influencing the results. As when using a pendulum, it's possible to unconsciously affect the movement of the *planchette* (the pointer) with imperceptible muscle movements through the ideomotor effect. To avoid this:

- Always sit at a board with someone you trust
- Record your session or ask a "scribe" to write questions and answers as they come up
- Rest your fingertips extremely lightly on the planchette—so lightly you can slide a piece of paper under your fingertips or shine a light underneath them and see it on the other side
- Release expectations

You can conduct Ouija or talking board sessions in the same manner:

1. You will need at least two and possibly three people for a session. Designate two people as the sitters and the third, if you have one, as the scribe.

2. Both sitters sit in chairs with their feet flat on the floor. Place the board between you, either balanced flat on both of your knees or on a small table.

3. The sitters hold their forearms up off the table or the board, parallel to the floor, and tuck their elbows into their sides, placing the middle three fingertips of each hand lightly on either side of the planchette.

4. Designate one of the sitters as the person who will ask the questions (the questioner).

5. When you are ready, the questioner states an affirmation or prayer. For example, "We are thankful for any positive spirits, angels, or guides who wish to answer our questions today. We are surrounded by the universal light of love and protection, and seek answers that serve the universal highest good."

6. Both sitters "warm up" the board by sliding the planchette three times in a clockwise circle, then return it to center.

7. The questioner asks questions. Allow plenty of time for spirits to answer— be patient. If nothing happens after about ten minutes, however, close your session and try again another time.

8. When you're done asking questions, close the session by offering thanks to all who have communicated and sliding the planchette to "goodbye" and then off the board. Turn the board over so the letters touch the table or your knees. Then, pack the board away with the planchette wrapped in fabric so it doesn't touch the board while it's stored in the box.

When working with a talking board, keep the following in mind:

- Always close the session as described in step 8, even if the board has been nonresponsive.

- If the pointer starts to count down from 9 to 0, go forward or backward through the alphabet, repeatedly slide back and forth between two letters, or slide to "goodbye" on its own, close the session. Do not continue.

- Close the board before changing sitters or questioner.

- Never leave a talking board sitting out—always close the door you have opened into the spirit world when you're done communicating.

- Always express your gratitude for those who have communicated with you.

NUMEROLOGY AND ANGEL NUMBERS

Numerology is a form of divination using numbers. Numbers have symbolic and significant meaning when they appear in your life in various forms.

Numerology offers interpretations for the numbers 0 through 9 as well as the numbers 11, 22, and 33. All other numbers are "reduced" until they become one of these numbers by adding them together. For example, if you're calculating the numerology of your house number, and your address is 4329, you would reduce this number as follows:

4+3+2+9=18

1+8=9

From here, you would look up the number 9 to determine what it suggests about your home.

You can use numerology for virtually anything, including as your date of birth and your birth name (after converting letters to numbers), and these will share important information about your life. Days, months, and years also have specific numerology associations that can provide guidance about the challenges you will face on a specific day, during a specific month, and so on. Numerology provides information about things such as karmic challenges, future events and issues, and more. It is a complex field of study, and there are many great texts you can use to either look up the numbers you encounter or learn how to work with numerology.

Angel numbers rely somewhat on numerology, but they go further. These are repeating patterns of numbers that you encounter frequently, such as repeatedly seeing 11:11 on a clock or waking up at 3:05 a.m. When you encounter these numbers, they offer messages of love and reassurance from those in the angelic realm indicating important life events, such as spiritual awakening, the presence of psychic ability, or reassurance you're on the right path. As with numerology, there are plenty of resources you can consult if you encounter angel numbers.

Both numerology numbers and angel numbers carry deep symbolism and may appear in any number of ways, such as in dreams, phone numbers, addresses, dates of birth, prices, and more. Keep an open mind and be aware of the numbers you come across. If you feel drawn to study numerology or angel numbers, consult the Resources for Psychics section for some starting points.

ASTROLOGY

Astrology is more than just the daily horoscopes you find online, in apps, or in the newspaper. Daily horoscopes focus on your *sun sign*, which is an indication of where the sun was in your astrological chart on the day of your birth.

However, sun signs are just one element of the sum total of your astrological influences. A natal chart is a complex calculation of where each of the planets was at the moment of your birth along with other factors. The position of each aspect of an astrological chart contributes to various aspects of your life, such as personality, love and partnership, work, family, health, finances, and more.

I love astrology for how accurate a full birth chart actually is; I have studied it quite extensively but still feel as if I have barely scratched the surface. Astrology provides information about the karmic challenges one faces throughout the present incarnation of their soul, but it's up to the individual to decide whether each aspect of their chart will have its most negative expression or its most positive.

Astrology requires study if you'd like to move beyond sun signs, which is essential for astrology to be beneficial. Visit the Resources for Psychics section for some great places to gain a better understanding of astrology.

DREAM INTERPRETATION

Many of your dreams come from your subconscious mind, your spirit guides, and your higher self. Learning to interpret your symbolic dreams can provide deep insight into yourself. Here are some of the different types of dreams you might encounter.

Processing Dreams

Processing dreams allow your sleeping mind to process the mundane details of your daily grind in order to sort your memories into their proper spots in your brain. These dreams usually seem insignificant, and many people don't remember them at all.

Prophetic Dreams

Prophetic dreams tell of things to come, whether in your personal life, for another person or group of people, or on a larger stage, such as worldwide events. These dreams tend to be extremely vivid.

Lucid Dreams

Lucid dreams are those in which you are aware you're dreaming and can control where you go and what you do in them. These are fun dreams because they allow you to have adventures, such as traveling or flying.

Visitation Dreams

Visitation dreams are when someone who has died (or a spirit guide) visits you while you're asleep. Like prophetic dreams, they have a hyperreal quality and are vivid and emotional.

Symbolic Dreams

Symbolic dreams are those that seem a little weird and often don't make a ton of sense because they're full of symbols. These are the dreams to interpret because they can provide insights into your life and show you opportunities for growth.

The symbols that appear in these dreams come from many sources, including the collective consciousness and personal, family, community, cultural, and religious symbolism. The best place to start when attempting to interpret a symbolic dream is to ask, "What does this dream mean to me?" or "What does this symbol mean to me?"

Start with your own personal symbolism; I find that for many, that's all they need to do because once they look at their dreams, they intuitively understand what they mean. If you think your dream has a specific meaning, you're probably right.

If, however, you just can't suss out the meaning of a dream, you can use a dream dictionary to help you interpret the various symbols. Write down everything you noticed in the dream, including people, items, colors, numbers, places, and action. Then, find a good dream dictionary to help you interpret it. This takes practice, but over time it becomes second nature.

Dream interpretation is a huge topic. For more information or to learn how to do it, see the Resources for Psychics section.

· ·

I hope you've discovered some psychic tools in this chapter that you feel drawn to. While you don't need *to use any of them, they provide a great way to focus and support your abilities.*

CHAPTER 6

Psychic Development Exercises and Games

E quipped with an understanding of how you receive and perceive psychic information, how to protect yourself, and which tools can be helpful, you're probably eager to start experimenting and working with your abilities.

One of my favorite classes to teach is something I like to call Psychic Game Night. It's a series of psychic exercises and games to help strengthen abilities so you can begin flexing and strengthening your psychic muscle. My students are often surprised to realize they're actually pretty good at picking up psychic sensory information, and they leave with a newfound sense of confidence and a number of exercises they can use to continue to work with their abilities.

Try these practices, games, and exercises. Spend a few minutes each day engaging in one or more of the activities that follow. It's a great way to begin to strengthen your psychic abilities—and to understand how you perceive and receive psychic energy and to strengthen the clairs where you may not be as strong. I know the longer I've worked with my abilities, the stronger my weaker psychic senses have become. In the beginning, I started out with my empathic, clairtangent, claircognizant, and clairsentient abilities being the strongest. As I've grown as a psychic over the past decades, my clairvoyant, clairaudient, clairgustant, and clairolfactant psychic senses have become just as strong as my initial abilities were.

PRACTICE MEDITATION AND PRESENCE

Perhaps the single most important thing to practice to develop your psychic senses is presence. For many, this means a regular meditation practice. However, before you panic, slam the book shut, and dismiss the idea out of hand, please hear me out.

For years, people told me, "You need to meditate if you want to grow as a healer and psychic." This was, I thought, one of my worst nightmares because I had (and to some extent still have) one of *those* brains. It yammers on incessantly, thinking, judging, and analyzing instead of resting in a state of calm readiness. If someone asks me, "What are you thinking right now?" and I answer, "Nothing," I'm lying. Never once in my entire life has there been nothing in my mind, although the cacophony that used to prevail has dimmed to a background murmur that allows me to focus on things other than my incessant thoughts.

Because of all this, I believed I couldn't meditate. No. I *knew* I couldn't. I tried—boy, did I try. I'd tried since I was a kid, and it had never worked for me. I would sit quietly, pretzeled into a lotus position, focusing on my breath and reminding myself to clear my mind. And pretty much the second I *thought* my mind had cleared, I would realize I was thinking about and congratulating myself that my mind was clear, which was a sure sign it wasn't clear because I was thinking. On and on it went, and the more frustrated I grew, the less beneficial the practice was for me.

And so, for me, as it is for many others, classic meditation was an exercise in frustration. Instead of focusing and relaxing me, it totally stressed me out, man. And because it stressed me out, it felt like a chore, which meant I avoided doing it.

Then, a wise teacher pointed out to me that perhaps it wasn't that I couldn't meditate but that I was defining meditation too narrowly. He reminded me that meditation wasn't so much about emptying my brain as it was about being present in the moment and noticing whatever sensory information presented itself. It's the end result of the mediation practice—presence—that matters, and not how you achieve that result. As they say, all roads lead to Rome; it doesn't matter which one you take as long as you get there in the end. A delightful or educational detour may take you away from your destination for a bit, but detours can be opportunities for learning, growth, and new experiences. Trust yourself, be patient, and enjoy the journey.

My expectation for meditation, not the practice itself, was the source of my discomfort. The goal was an empty mind, something I have never once achieved in my entire life, and so I needed to shift that expectation into something that was possible and manageable for me, and I find this to be true for others as well.

What I now understand about meditation is that it doesn't necessarily mean my brain will be a ghost town with tumbleweeds blowing through. Instead, when I engage in meditation and presence activities, my mind is alert, focused on the present moment, and in a state of allowing in order to create space for higher wisdom and knowledge to enter. This involves quieting my internal dialogue, the voice that chatters on about what will happen in the future or what has happened in the past.

If we keep our brains jam-packed with thoughts about the past and future, spinning stories about what has already happened to us or anticipating what might happen, then how can we be fully present to notice what is happening right now? The answer is "Not easily." And being present is essential for both allowing space for psychic sensory information to arise and noticing when it does. The goal, then, isn't total annihilation of every thought you have, but rather management of those thoughts so you can be aware of what is happening right now in this very moment.

Classic Meditation

If you are someone who is able to enter a quiet, focused meditative state through traditional meditation practices, then by all means keep at those.

1. Go somewhere you won't be disturbed.

2. Sit quietly with the bottoms of your feet flat on the floor for grounding (see page 83) and make yourself comfortable.

3. Notice your breathing, taking breaths in through your nose and out through your mouth. If it helps, focus on your breathing and return your attention to your breath every time your mind wanders.

4. Allow thoughts to flow through your mind. When they do, notice them and then allow them to gently drift away. Some people find it helps to use imagery to release their thoughts, such as visualizing a broom sweeping them away or saying "erase" and watching them disappear. Find imagery that works for you.

5. Do this for ten to fifteen minutes or longer.

It may be helpful to play white noise or peaceful music and to use a meditation cushion to help make you more comfortable. Some people also like to diffuse essential oils that assist in achieving meditative states, such as frankincense, lavender, or sandalwood.

If you struggle with traditional practices like this, however, all is not lost. There are a number of practices you can try until you land on one or a few that work for you.

Living Meditation

Living meditation, something I call *presencing*, is the practice of focusing on sensory information as you go about daily activities instead of getting lost in your thoughts. Of course, you can't do this all the time; sometimes you have to think (such as when you're driving your car or doing your job). However, when you're engaged in other tasks that don't require much thought—such as cleaning the house, listening to music, doing dishes, or eating—instead of spending all that time thinking, pay attention to your senses. I'll use showering as an example to give you an idea, since showering is a highly sensory experience.

Showering is just one example of sensory presencing. I find opportunities to do this throughout the day. One of my favorites is when I drink cold water; I love to pay

The presencing version of a shower might look something like this:

- Before stepping into the shower, notice the sensation of the air on your skin.

- Notice the sound of the water as you turn it on and as it strikes the shower floor.

- Watch the steam rise from the water and see the droplets splash as they hit the floor.

- When you step into the shower, notice the warmth on your skin and the difference from how it felt while you were standing outside of it. Feel the slippery tiles under your bare feet.

- Close your eyes under the shower and feel the intensity of the water droplets striking your head and shoulders. Feel the rivulets of water running down the sides of your face and down your back and front.

- As you wash yourself, notice aromas and textures. Allow yourself the full experience of the shower. For example, notice how the sensation changes when you wash your skin with soap versus when you are rinsing it with water. Notice the aroma of your shampoo when you open the bottle and how it changes when it comes in contact with the water.

- If you feel other thoughts intruding, notice them and then release them, returning your focus to your senses.

attention to the flavor of the water and how it feels as the cold liquid takes the journey from my mouth to my stomach. It's a very satisfying way to drink water.

Living meditation is easy for anyone to practice, and it's helpful in learning to quiet your mind and focus on sensory data. This is important for psychic development because psychic sensory information also comes through your senses—your psychic senses rather than your physical ones, but the neurological connection is the same. When your mind is focused and alert, you are more open to receiving information.

Movement Meditation

Another of my favorite meditative practices for nonmeditators is movement meditation. When I'm moving, I can set aside my thoughts and instead focus on my movements, on how those movements feel in my body, and on other sensory data.

Movement meditation can be as easy as taking a walk and paying attention to what you see, smell, hear, and feel. As you walk, focus on your breathing, notice sensations in your body, feel the ground underneath your feet, and view the world around you through new eyes and the beginner's mind. Pay attention and notice things you've never noticed before.

You have other options for meditative movement practices as well. I enjoy yoga and Nia (a form of dance exercise), which both bring me straight into the present moment. Other practices that work for movement meditation include running, dancing, martial arts, paddleboarding or rowing, bicycling, swimming, and any other form of movement you enjoy.

Single-Sense Presencing

There are as many ways of meditating as there are people practicing meditation. One that many people find relatively easy is to focus on one physical sense at a time. Sight and sound are the most common, although if you're highly kinesthetic, then you can also use touch. To practice single-sense presencing, go someplace where you won't be disturbed and minimize sensory information as much as possible by dimming the lights and playing white noise in the background. Then, focus on a single sense.

Some things you can try:

- Sit in a dark, quiet room and gaze at a candle flame. When your mind wanders, bring your attention back to the flame.

- Use headphones to listen to binaural beats, which are special frequencies that can affect brain waves in various ways and help to move you into a meditative state.

- Stroke a pet or an object with a texture you find pleasing.

- Sit in the sun and feel the sensation of sunlight and the breeze playing on your skin.

- Watch autonomous sensory meridian response (ASMR) videos, which use certain (usually soft) sounds to create a tingling sensation and a light form of self-hypnosis.

- Burn herbs or incense or diffuse essential oils and focus on your sense of smell.

Additional Meditative Practices

I do meditate formally now because I found that as I focused on having more sensory presence in my life and using the preceding techniques, the practice of formal meditation became easier for me. I started with about five minutes per session, and now I can go for much longer if I have the time to do so. However, I recommend that even if you do engage in traditional forms of meditation, you also seek as many opportunities as possible to be present. For example:

- When you eat, focus only on the sensations of smelling, tasting, chewing, and swallowing instead of carrying on a conversation, watching television, or thinking. See how much you can notice about the foods you eat.

- When having a conversation with someone, practice being present and using deep listening. Instead of thinking about what you will say next or how you will respond, pay attention to what the other person is telling you. Notice their body language, the tone of their voice, how their eyes look, and their microexpressions as well as what they're telling you.

- Occasionally throughout the day, pause for a few moments, plant your feet firmly on the floor, place both hands over your heart, and take several deep breaths. Inhale through your nose for a count of four, hold for a count of four, and exhale through your mouth for a count of four.

- Try prerecorded guided meditations of visualizations.

ASK FOR AND RECORD PSYCHIC DREAMS

When we are unable to tune in to psychic information during the day, our higher selves and guides don't give up. Instead, they attempt to send us information while we sleep, when our minds are more receptive to it. This is why some people who claim to have zero psychic abilities when they are awake may have vivid and profound psychic dreams while they sleep.

You can influence your dreams before you go to bed by stating your intention to receive information in your dreams. I do this simply by saying before I drift off to sleep every night, "Tell me what I need to know." You can do this if it works for you, or you can recite any prayer, affirmation, or mantra as a statement of intention.

Many people tell me they don't have dreams, but I assure them they do—they just don't remember them. If you don't remember your dreams when you wake, then you may also want to include an affirmation about remembering your dreams. So, before you go to sleep, you might affirm, "Tonight as I sleep, I will receive the information that serves my greatest good in my dreams, and I will remember the information when I wake."

Another affirmation I like to use is "Tonight, I will sleep comfortably, peacefully, and soundly. Spirit will tell me what I know in my dreams, and in the morning, I will awake refreshed, energized, and fully aware of the messages I received from Spirit."

One of the reasons we struggle to remember our dreams after we wake is because they are so ephemeral in nature. If we don't record them right away, then we are likely to forget them. For people who simply cannot remember their dreams, or who know they dream but wake up and can't recall what happened during their sleep, I recommend keeping a notepad or voice recorder next to the bed. As soon as you wake, record any dreams, thoughts, or impressions.

I suggest doing this even in the middle of the night if you can easily go back to sleep afterward. My friend Traci did this at my suggestion, and she showed me her notepad with her middle-of-the-night scribblings in it. She wakes up from a dream and leaves the lights off but hastily scribbles a word or two on the pad to trigger her memories in the morning. She reports it hasn't negatively affected her sleep, and it has increased her awareness of her dreams and her ability to remember them.

LEARN TO SENSE ENERGY

Building your psychic senses can be a lot of fun. I have a number of games I teach my students that help them to build their psychic senses. Many over the years have expressed their certainty that there was no way they'd be able to "pick up" anything, and yet I've never seen a student who wasn't pleasantly surprised when one or more of these activities showed them that they did, indeed, have at least some level of psychic sensory ability.

Hand Scan

The hand scan is a fun way to play with psychometry and clairtangency. I've taught this in a number of psychic and energy healing workshops, and it's always a hit. In the beginning, I recommend you do this activity with a trusted friend as a partner so you can receive verbal feedback. Once you've got it dialed in, you can then practice on objects, plants, and animals as well.

Before you begin, I want you to experience what the sensation of energy feels like in your hands, so do the following:

1. Rub the palms of your hands vigorously together to build up friction until they get good and hot.

2. Now, keeping your hands parallel with palms facing each other, slowly pull them apart, noticing the tingling between them.

3. Continue to pull them apart until you feel the separation from that tingly energy.

4. Now, slowly move them back toward each other until you can feel the energy between them again. See whether you can locate where the edge of that energy is—move your hands together and apart until you can tell when the energy is there and when it isn't.

Once you've done this a few times and understand what the energy feels like, have your partner stand in front of you with their back to you.

1. Starting at your partner's head and working down the midline of their body, hold your hand with your palm facing them, three to five inches away from their body, and slowly sweep your hand down without touching it.

2. As you move your hand, pay attention to its sensations. You may notice subtle differences, such as pressure, pushing, pulling, hot, cold, tingling, or deadness.

3. When you get to a spot where you notice a change in sensation, tell your partner what you feel and ask for feedback as to whether they notice anything in that spot.

Many of my students receive significant confirmation from their partner that what they're noticing is accurate.

Empathy Practice

You can hone your empathy, and possibly your clairtangency, by working with a trusted partner as well. It's important for this exercise that you work with someone you trust implicitly in order to keep you energetically safe.

Before you begin, don't ask your partner anything about their current feelings, how their day has been, or anything else along those lines. You want to go into this exercise with as blank of a slate as you can. You will need a blindfold and either headphones with noise canceling or those playing white noise for this exercise.

1. Sit comfortably with either your feet or bottom flat on the ground.

2. Put on the blindfold and headphones.

3. Have your partner enter the room and sit facing you.

4. Once they are seated, have your partner reach out and take your hand without speaking. Now, pay attention and see what you notice.
   - What thoughts arise?
   - Do you see any images in your mind's eye?
   - Do you "hear" anything?
   - Do you feel any differences in emotions?
   - Do you notice any sensations in your body associated with discomfort, pain, tingling, etc.?

5. Sit this way for five to ten minutes simply attending to what you notice without judgment.

6. Then, remove your blindfold and headphones and share with your partner the things you noticed.

7. Allow your partner to provide feedback.

Sensing Energy in Your Body

Whenever I teach this in my classes, I demonstrate it first, which always evokes a laugh from my students. Apparently watching a middle-aged mom assuming a martial arts stance and yelling "Heeeyahhh!" while punching the air is amusing. However, it's also super powerful because it teaches you how to sense energy in your body.

You can practice this alone or with others. The more people who practice together, the greater the collective energy buildup from each activity (making it easier to sense). I choose martial arts moves because the two different styles I demonstrate have distinctly different energies that are easy to sense in your body. This only takes a minute or two, but you can do it as many times as you wish to notice the difference in sensation.

1. Stand with your feet flat on the floor under your hips and your knees slightly bent.

2. Hold your arms in a "ready" position with your elbows tucked into your sides, bent at a 90-degree angle with your forearms parallel to the floor, palms facing up, and hands curled very lightly into fists.

3. Take a few deep breaths, grounding firmly into the ground. When you're ready, briskly and firmly step out to the side with your right foot at the same time as you punch quickly and strongly forward with the heel of your right hand. As you do, yell "Heyah!" or whatever other strong, loud vocalization feels right to you. Don't worry about form here or doing it "right." Simply perform a bold, aggressive, karate-like move as if you were striking someone and add a loud, aggressive vocalization. Return to the ready position.

4. Stand for a minute with your eyes closed and notice how that energy feels in your body. Repeat this sequence a few times if you need to get a handle on the sensation.

5. Now, standing in the ready position, close your eyes, ground, and breathe deeply again.

6. When you're ready, make a tai chi–style move, stepping to the side in a gentle, flowing manner with your right foot, following with both arms in a flowing, gentle motion as if you are pushing a big bubble of air and then gathering it as you step back into the ready position. As you do, softly say "Aaaaaaaaahhhhhh," like a deep, pleasurable sigh. Do this a few times.

7. Stand in the ready position and notice how this feels in your body.

8. Again, don't worry as much about making a proper martial arts motion. Instead simply make a smooth, gentle, soft, flowing motion as opposed to the aggressive, percussive, loud, karate-style motion you did before.

These two motions both move *chi* (life force energy) in your body, but they have different results in how your body senses that motion. Pay close attention to the energetic sensations you feel as you complete each move. You can try this with other combinations of gentle and aggressive movements as well. For example, try some smooth, slow, ballet-style dance movements followed by some energetic cancan-style dance kicks.

Who's Behind Me?

If you're in a group, you can try to sense the energy of an unknown person behind you. This game teaches you to recognize the difference in everyone's energy signature or vibe. Every person's vibe is slightly different. These subtle differences have always been clear to me because it's a gift that has been with me my entire life, but for other people, it's a muscle that needs to be exercised to get stronger. The more you practice sensing other people's vibes, the better you'll get at it.

You'll need a group of at least three people; more are better. You'll also need a chair, a blindfold, and headphones with noise canceling or those playing white noise. The participants can take turns being the sitter.

1. Have the sitter sit in a chair with their feet flat on the floor, ideally in a separate room from the other participants, wearing the blindfold and headphones.

2. One at a time, each of the other participants walks into the room behind the sitter and gently touches them on the shoulder to let the sitter know they're there.

3. That person steps back and stands a few feet directly behind the sitter.

4. As the sitter, pay attention to the energy and name who you think it is.

5. Repeat for each other person, allowing them to enter the room one at a time, touch the sitter on the shoulder, and stand behind them.

6. At the end, each person who entered the room can confirm to the sitter whether they sensed correctly.

Don't get discouraged if you're not successful right away. This takes some practice and some level of familiarity with the people involved, but eventually sitters become more proficient at sensing other's vibes. It's also important to note that some people's energy is more contained than others. For example, my husband's energy is extremely contained and subtle. He's one of the few people who can actually sneak up on me because I can't feel him coming, which may actually be one of the things that initially attracted me to him—it was so different from anything I'd felt before, and it felt peaceful to me.

Energy Ball

You'll need a willing partner for this game, which helps you learn to sense energy as it comes at you. Essentially, you'll be playing a game of catch with an invisible ball of energy.

1. Stand facing your partner, both of you with your eyes closed.

2. Designate who will start the game.

3. The person designated rubs their hands together until static builds up and then pulls them apart slightly to create a ball of energy between their hands.

4. The other partner stands with their hands held out in front of them, ready to catch the ball.

5. When the designated partner is ready, toss the ball to the other participant.

6. If you're the partner, focus on your hands. You should feel a slight sensation of energy (or a major one) hit your hands when they toss the ball.

7. Say something such as "Caught it!" and allow your partner to confirm they have tossed it. Toss it back to your partner.

8. Go back and forth in this way. With practice, you'll become more adept at sensing when your partner throws the ball and the energy hits your hands.

Charged Crystals

This is a powerful demonstration I offer in virtually every one of my classes. It's based on the principles discovered by Masaru Emoto, who charged water with positive and negative messages taped to water containers, such as "I love you" and "I hate you." After exposing the water to these messages, Emoto photographed ice crystals made from the water and found that the shapes of the crystals had extreme variations based on the messages. Harmonious, loving messages created beautiful, ordered crystals, while negative, hateful messages created brown, ugly, chaotic structures. It was a powerful demonstration.

Based on this, I decided to try it with crystals and was surprised at how easily my students could sense the difference when they held the crystals in their hand. To do this, you'll need two identical crystals (I recommend round clear quartz beads), two zipper bags, two slips of paper, and a pen or pencil.

1. On one slip of paper, write "I love you."

2. Fold it so you can't read it and toss it in one of the zipper bags with one of the crystals.

3. On the other slip, write "I hate you."

4. Fold it and put it in the other zipper bag with the other crystal.

5. Ask someone to mix up the bags so you don't know which is which.

6. Leave the bags to sit for at least forty-eight hours.

7. Remove the crystals from the bags, keeping in mind which came from which bag so you can go back and check your results.

8. Hold the crystals, one at a time, in your receiving hand, which is your nondominant hand (left if you're right-handed or right if you're left-handed).

9. Close your eyes and pay attention to the sensations. Can you feel a difference in the crystals? Which do you think is which? Make your guess, then check on the papers.

10. Cleanse the "I hate you" crystal with palo santo smoke to dissipate the negative energy when you're done.

This is another one that gets easier with practice, but it's a great way to learn to feel energy.

PLAY WITH CARDS

You can use various types of cards to develop clairvoyance and telepathy. While parapsychologists use a dedicated type of card called *Zener cards* for working with clairvoyance and telepathy, you don't need to get a special deck—a standard deck of playing cards will also work.

Solo Playing Card Exercise

For this exercise, which can help you with developing the psychic sense of clairvoyance and claircognizance, you will need a standard, unmarked deck of fifty-two playing cards.

1. Sit comfortably with the playing cards in a pile facedown in front of you.

2. Place your hand on the top card, close your eyes, take a deep breath, and say the first thing that comes to mind: red or black.

3. Turn the card over. If you're correct, place it in one pile. If you're incorrect, place it in another.

4. Continue through the deck. If you have more than twenty-six cards in the "correct" pile, you're functioning above chance (you have a one in two chance of guessing a card correctly).

5. After you're consistently doing well with this challenge, do the same thing but this time guessing suits. In this case, if you have more than thirteen cards in your correct pile, you're operating above chance (you have a one in four chance of guessing a card correctly).

6. You can progress to guessing number on the face of the card and, ultimately, guessing the specific card. Some people become very proficient at this. For example my former husband could do it at about 80 percent proficiency for guessing the exact card.

Partner Playing Card Exercise

You can do the above exercise with a partner as well. Have the partner focus on the card while they look at it. Close your eyes and say the first thing that comes to mind. This can help build telepathic communication.

Zener Card Exercise

Zener cards are an instrument researchers use to test psychics, but you can also use them as a psychic development tool. There twenty-five cards in a Zener deck with five different symbols on cards as shown on the opposite page.

You can use Zener cards in the same way you'd use playing cards, either alone or with a partner. Close your eyes and see if you can come up with the correct image. Sort into correct and incorrect piles. You have a one in five chance of being correct, so if you have more than five correct cards in your correct pile, you are operating above chance.

When I work with Zener cards, typically the full image of the card pops into my mind, although sometimes I'll hear "star" or know "cross" or "noodles" (that's what I call the squiggly lines). One odd thing that frequently happens to me with Zener cards is I am a card ahead of the card I'm holding; I'll guess the card in my hand wrong, but it's inevitably the next card I hold. I have no idea why that happens, but it's a consistent thing with me.

You can also find online Zener card games and tests. See the Resources for Psychics section for information.

Psychic Memory Card Game

This is another popular game in my classes, and I'm always amazed at how well people do with it. For the game, you'll need a children's memory card game with simple images on it and several envelopes. This can help with clairvoyance and remote viewing. To play:

1. Separate the pairs so you only have one card with each picture. Set the other halves of the pairs aside.

2. Place the cards facedown and shuffle them well.

3. Keeping the cards facedown so you can't see them, place one in each envelope and seal them.

4. Shuffle the envelopes.

5. Hold each envelope in your hand in turn. Close your eyes and notice what images you see. Write the properties of each thing you see on the back of the envelope, such as "orange," "round," "curve," "plant," "animal," and so on.

6. Open the envelopes and see how close what you saw is to the actual image.

I find that people are more likely to see elements of the image versus the whole image, so they might notice an animal shape, a shape with lots of curves, or specific colors. With time, they develop a better ability to see the entire image.

A variation on this is to place one card of each pair facedown on a table in front of you. Draw one of the cards from the pile containing the other halves of the pairs, look at it, and see if you can sense where its match is.

Photo and Shape Game

You can take the memory card game above and apply it to photographs as well. It helps to have someone else provide the photographs already in envelopes instead of using your own. For a simpler version, have someone cut basic shapes from different colors of construction paper and put them into sealed envelopes.

PSYCHOMETRY PRACTICE

To practice psychometry, you'll need a friend to bring you a few objects they know something about that you don't. The objects can have a specific story attached to them, or they can just be something someone they know handles and uses a lot so it has their energy on it.

To play:

1. Sit comfortably with your feet flat on the floor. Take a few deep breaths to ground and center.

2. Hold the object in your receiving (nondominant) hand. Close your eyes. Notice what comes to mind.

3. Say what you notice without interpretation or editing.

4. Have your partner wait until you are done before they confirm or deny elements of what you sensed.

You can also play more difficult version of this game by placing the object in a box so you can't see it and holding the box. This can remove any predetermined biases you might have from seeing the object. As with other games, people tend to improve with practice, so start simply, don't get discouraged, and work your way up to greater difficulty.

STUDY PSYCHIC SYMBOLS

As previously mentioned, a lot of psychic information (especially if you're a medium) comes not literally but symbolically. This can make it a challenge to understand the information you receive, but it's not insurmountable.

I find that psychic symbolism is similar to dream symbols because they come from the same source. Therefore, if you're familiar with one type of symbol, you'll also be familiar with the other. I recommend purchasing either a dream dictionary or a psychic symbol dictionary; my favorite free online resource is the Dream Moods website.

However, keep in mind the following when working with psychic symbols:

- Symbols may vary from psychic to psychic because personal, familial, community, cultural, and religions symbolism vary from person to person.

- Psychic symbols may be more than just visual. Symbolic psychic language can affect any of your senses. Some examples:

  · The taste of blood may indicate a violent death

  · The aroma of roses may indicate love

  · The color pink may indicate compassion

  · The sound of a gavel may indicate justice

I can't tell you what other people's personal symbolism may be (or what yours is), but I can help you understand more of what to pay attention to by sharing a few symbols that come from my work as a medium, which is the work through which I tend to receive the majority of the psychic symbols I notice.

- The smell of ozone or pressure in my ears indicates a spirit is present.

- Tightness in a certain part of my body indicates the likely manner of death (for example, tightness in my chest may indicate heart issues).

- Dizziness and headaches indicate some type of head issue such as aneurysm or stroke.

- Sudden blackness indicates sudden death.

- The sensation of a tug on a pant leg indicates the presence of a child spirit.

- Dampening of my hearing indicates there were communication problems in life with the living person they were communicating with.

- Hearing a bell or a chime indicates the spirit wishes to apologize or acknowledge another's apology.

- A buzzing sound in my ears indicates anger or frustration at the time of death or a spirit who isn't at peace

- Seeing white roses indicates remorse for actions in life.

- Seeing wavy lines similar to heat haze indicates that another spirit wants to come through.

- The smell of sulfur indicates a person did bad or evil things in life.

- I see numbers quite a lot, but they can be a bit tricky. Numbers typically represent a date, a month, or a specified period of time (such as a number of weeks). It can also indicate the age when the person died, or it may be associated with the numerology meaning or another significant event in the spirit's life (for example, I might see a four and discover the spirit had four children).

- Instead of a full name, I typically get a sense of "sounds like." Usually, I can "hear" consonants, but vowels are more difficult. So, for someone named Amanda, for instance, I might know it's an "Am" name with a "d" in it, or for Martin, I might know it's a "Mar" name. These are accurate as long as I relay them exactly and don't try to fill in the rest of the letters. If I fill in the rest of the letters myself, I'm inevitably wrong.

- I often see symbols associated with occupations, such as a clerical collar, a hammer, or a blackboard. While I can generally interpret these as, for example, minister, construction worker, or teacher, I typically relay the symbol instead because sometimes the image is a symbol representing something similar but not quite the same.

- If I hear the sound of skittering feet, it represents that the spirit of a pet is present.

These are just a few of the many ways spirits may communicate with me symbolically. Of course, the information can be more straightforward as well. I've seen people's cars and houses, heard names and numbers, smelled cigarette smoke and perfume, and other things that require little to no interpretation.

• •

It can be a lot of fun to learn how your psychic abilities work and play with them to discover new gifts and develop those you have. I highly recommend trying some of the techniques and practices in this chapter if you wish to grow as a psychic.

Moving forward into the next chapter, we're going to switch gears and explore the unique experiences of people with empathic psychic abilities as well as provide coping strategies so if you're an empath, you can feel safe, secure, and at peace with your abilities.

CHAPTER 7

Coping Strategies for Empaths

While empathy is one of the clairs and a natural psychic gift, it can be one of the more difficult abilities to cope with. I'm highly empathic and have been since I was young. In fact, I'm certain it is one of the main reasons I experienced so much anxiety before I learned to control my psychic abilities.

Empaths often struggle because they pick up the emotions and physical sensations of others and experience them as if they are their own. Therefore, empaths often require additional coping strategies and tools to help them manage these physical and emotional sensations.

EMPATHY: GIFT OR CURSE?

I used to refer to empathy as my greatest gift and my greatest curse. I felt it was a gift because it allowed me to connect deeply with others and served as my source of compassion. On the other hand, because I am both emotionally and physically empathic, before I understood what it was, why it was happening, and how to control it, my empathy also caused me a lot of physical and emotional pain. Since I've learned to work with my empathy, however, I now identify it as my greatest gift, and I no longer feel it's a curse. It has helped me be a better daughter, sister, wife, mother, friend, psychic, and energy healer.

UNIQUE CHALLENGES OF BEING EMPATHIC

Many of the challenges associated with being empathic arise when you aren't entirely aware you have this gift or when you don't manage it in appropriate ways. Because empaths tend to feel and own everything that goes on around them, they often experience unique challenges.

Challenges for Clairtangent Empaths

Clairtangent empaths (also sometimes called *physical empaths*) frequently feel the physical symptoms of others simply by being in their proximity, although being near someone isn't required to trigger physical symptoms. As a physical empath, you might also experience the physical symptoms of a loved one who is far away but with whom you share an energetic connection, or you might inadvertently connect with someone's energy and physical symptoms simply from seeing them on television or encountering them on social media.

When you go someplace public, you may experience a whole host of passing or lingering unpleasant physical symptoms that you didn't notice before you left the house. This occurs because you are picking up the physical ailments of people around you, but these symptoms feel as if they belong to you; it's virtually impossible from a physical standpoint to differentiate another person's symptoms from your own. For example, when I was about eight years old, my family went to the Spokane

EMPATHY SELF-ASSESSMENT

I briefly outlined the qualities of being empathic in chapter 2, but here, I offer a more in-depth analysis to help you determine whether you're an empath. The more statements you respond yes to, the more strongly empathic you are, and the more benefit you will receive from the coping strategies in this chapter. Keep in mind that empathic abilities can grow, so your responses will likely change over time. If you identify with five or more of the statements here, you likely have some degree of clairempathy. The more yes answers you have, the more strongly you are affected by your empathic gifts.

Statement	Check If Yes
I frequently experience emotions that seem to come out of nowhere.	
I would classify myself as an anxious person.	
I have been diagnosed with an anxiety disorder.	
My emotions are all over the place when I'm in a crowd.	
I feel more anxious or emotional when I'm in public.	
I feel less anxious or emotional when I am home alone.	
When someone else cries, I cry.	
Silly things make me cry, such as commercials or sporting events.	
I have mood swings I don't understand.	
I am attracted to difficult or challenging life partners.	
I can tell how someone is feeling the second they walk in a room.	
I become deeply absorbed and invested in novels, movies, or television shows.	
My emotions are often disconnected from what is happening in my life.	
In relationships, my partner's needs are always more important than mine.	
In relationships, my partner's feelings are always more important than mine.	
I often feel sad or depressed for no apparent reason.	
I find other people's anger overwhelming.	
When I'm around large groups, I experience strange symptoms, such as random aches and pains.	
I feel like life is one big emotional roller coaster.	
I can tell someone is ill before they know it.	
I tend to attract narcissists for friendships and relationships.	
When a relationship or friendship ends, I blame myself.	
I can't stand consuming violence as entertainment, such as in movies or sports.	
When I witness someone being physically or emotionally harmed, even a fictional person, I experience significant emotional distress.	

continued

When someone in my life is sick, I have the same physical symptoms they do, even if I am not ill myself.	
Being with emotionally closed-off or guarded people makes me feel safe.	
I can immediately sense the vibe of a room when I walk into it.	
People often share their darkest secrets with me.	
I'm often excited about social plans when I make them but dread following through as the time draws nearer.	
People tell me I'm oversensitive.	
My parents tell me I was an anxious baby.	
Pets make me feel calmer and more grounded.	
Intimate relationships feel so overwhelming that I either become enmeshed or seek to create distance.	
I can always tell when someone is lying to me.	
I have no tolerance for someone who seems fake or disingenuous.	
Being around certain people leaves me feeling drained.	
I'm a social chameleon and can easily adapt to people I spend a lot of time with, taking on their mannerisms and modes of speech.	
Nature has an immediate and calming effect on me.	
I am a natural caregiver and step in to help without being asked. If someone is hurting, I am compelled to help.	
I am drawn to mental, emotional, physical, and spiritual healing arts.	
I feel like an introvert inside, even if others see me as being highly sociable.	
Too much sensory information is overstimulating.	
I was often physically ill as a child.	
When I attend a crowded event, such as a festival or conference, I need several days afterward to recover.	
I have multiple chemical or food sensitivities.	
My doctors have diagnosed me with some type of "syndrome" because they can't make sense of my various symptoms (or they tell me it's all in my head).	
I have an autoimmune disease or some other chronic illness, such as fibromyalgia.	
I'm extremely picky about the texture of the fabrics I wear or touch frequently.	
I have developed an unhealthy adaptive response to stress, such as drinking or overeating.	
I use drugs, alcohol, or other behaviors to numb myself.	
I startle easily.	
My primary method of dealing with negativity is to socially isolate.	
Seeing an injured or dead animal is extremely distressing.	
I become highly distressed if I feel I have hurt someone's feelings.	
I am a people pleaser.	
TOTAL YES ANSWERS:	

World's Fair. It was packed with people, and the second we set foot on the fairgrounds, I started to feel ill. Throughout our visit to the fair, I had headaches, dizziness, light-headedness, nausea, and a host of other symptoms. As soon as we left, I felt fine.

As a result of experiencing so many physical symptoms, people who are clairtangent empaths often go on strange medical journeys featuring a host of unrelated symptoms that doctors can't quite pin down. Because of this, many physical empaths are diagnosed with a vague syndrome versus a specific disease; doctors often diagnose syndromes based on clusters of symptoms with a potential common cause. For example, in my early twenties I was diagnosed with chronic fatigue syndrome, which at the time my doctors guessed was associated with Epstein-Barr virus from a bout of mononucleosis I had when I was in college. I can recognize now with the benefit of hindsight that these physical issues were a result of my physical empathy; at the time, I worked in a busy gym and lived in a crowded apartment complex, so I was around lots of people every single day.

Some challenges physical empaths encounter include:

- Lots of childhood illnesses

- Frequent bouts of illnesses as an adult that are difficult to diagnose

- Sensitivity, allergy, or intolerance to ingested chemicals, drugs, or food additives (for example, I have celiac disease, am allergic to dairy products, and have extreme reactions to many medications)

- Airborne and food allergies or hypersensitivity to poor air quality

- Nonspecific aches and pains

- Chronic aches and pains

- Inflammation with no apparent cause

- Migraines or other headaches

- Chronic exhaustion

- Autoimmune disease

- Medical diagnosis of hypochondria

Challenges for Emotional Empaths

Emotional empaths also face challenges, mainly based on experiencing others' emotional states as if they are their own.

Challenges may include:

- Uncontrolled anxiety or diagnosed anxiety disorders not mitigated by medication or therapy (up to and including panic attacks)

- Phobias

- Toxic or difficult relationships and friendships

- Difficulty being in a crowd

- Difficulty living on a busy street, in a crowded neighborhood, or in multifamily housing

- Chronic physical and emotional exhaustion

- Becoming immediately drained in social situations

- Requiring long periods to recover after spending time in crowds

- Frequently feeling sad, down, or depressed

- Mood swings

- Being taking advantage of

- Difficulty saying no

- Addictive or numbing behaviors

- Struggles with health or body image

- Poor boundaries

- Being labeled as "overdramatic"

HOW EMPATHY IS A GIFT

Because the negative aspects of being an empath come to the fore when you don't recognize your empathic abilities, many people feel being empathic is a huge challenge and don't recognize the benefits inherent in these abilities. However, when you learn to work with your empathy instead of fighting it, numbing it, or ignoring it, it can become one of your greatest gifts.

I used to feel "cursed" by my empathy, mostly because I didn't understand it and because all I knew about it was that it frequently made me feel physically and emotionally uncomfortable. In fact, it made me so uncomfortable I would do anything I could to numb the feelings, which led to self-destructive behaviors.

However, as I started working with my empathy (and my other psychic abilities), I began to recognize just what a gift it is.

If you are an empath, some of the benefits of your gift include the following:

- It serves a source of deep compassion and caring for others
- You have a built-in lie detector and can tell when someone is being untruthful
- People are drawn to you, and you can experience deep and meaningful relationships
- Children and animals love you, and you take great joy from being around them
- You have a deep connection with nature and compassion for the planet
- Your empathy can become a driving force for social justice and compassionate action
- You feel the positive emotions of others, so if you're around somebody who is feeling fantastic, you're naturally uplifted as well
- Empathy provides a great advantages to those in the healing arts who have a natural instinct for helping clients and patients
- You can sense when a situation is about to go bad and remove yourself

PROTECTION FOR EMPATHS

So, how can you embrace the positive while minimizing the negative aspects of empathy? The answer is the same whether you are physically empathic, emotionally empathic, or both: practice good emotional and energetic self-care. There are a number of techniques you can enlist to help you be able to manage your abilities and make them a force for good in your life.

Setting Boundaries

Empaths are people pleasers. Why? Because when we feel someone else's pain as our own, we immediately want to mitigate it—to help them feel better so we can feel better. How this manifests in real life, however, is that empaths frequently have mushy boundaries; we have difficulty setting boundaries and even more maintaining them.

This is one of the reasons empaths may find themselves in friendships and relationships with people who take energy from others to nourish themselves, leaving the other person depleted—you may see them described as "emotional vampires." Empaths believe they can help; along with being people pleasers, they are fixers and often choose relationships with people they have a deep desire to "fix." In turn, emotional vampires are drawn to those whose boundaries they can easily override and whose energy they can easily take to supplement their own. It's an unhealthy parasitic relationship model that repeatedly plays out in the lives of many empaths.

Therefore, learning to set and maintain firm boundaries is an essential exercise for all empaths; it's not something we do naturally, so it needs to be a learned and practiced behavior. Because setting boundaries doesn't come naturally to empaths, it will take a little work to determine what your boundaries are. Once you do that, however, you can deploy strategies to maintain them.

Start by determining where your boundaries currently sit, realizing that boundaries are fluid and evolve over time, so you may need to reassess from time to time.

- Make a list of the emotional experiences you've had in your life that you didn't enjoy, such as toxic relationships, broken friendships, and so on.

- Ask, "What was my role in these? How am I the common denominator?"

- Ask yourself what emotional boundaries you could have set to avoid these situations. When could you have said no instead of saying yes?

- Now, consider the things currently in your life that make you feel anger or dissatisfaction. List all of them, even those that seem relatively minor, such as "I hate that I always have to do the dishes even though my family members say they will."

- Which of these can you change by saying no? Which are meaningful and matter to you?

Once you've taken your measure, choose one boundary that you aren't currently enforcing that it feels safe to set and come up with strategies for setting it. Then, work on just that boundary.

I'll provide you some insight into this process with a personal story. I have historically had poor boundaries. As a result, I've often been an easy target for bullies and narcissists. My experience has been that I tend toward fluid boundaries with these types of people until they bump up against one that is firm, such as violating my ethical code. As soon as someone does this, I dig in hard. The result is that the other person becomes extremely angry because I've never set a boundary with them before, and the relationship often goes down in flames.

This is a pattern that has repeated in my life, so I've spent a great deal of time reviewing it and discovering how to keep it from happening again. The common denominator I discovered was that early in the friendship or relationship, when something small came up that I didn't like, such as a negative comment I failed to address or an activity I truly didn't want to engage in but did anyway to keep the peace, I let it slide instead of enforcing my boundary. Therefore, I decided this was my first task: to not let something I perceived as small slide when I felt it violated one of my boundaries.

One of the places I first practiced this was on social media, where I felt it was relatively safe because I could carefully consider my response to someone pushing a boundary before I reacted. I noticed I had one friend who would only comment on my posts if they contained something she disagreed with. Disagreeing with me was fine—I'm okay with differences of opinion—but her responses felt rude, bullying, and dismissive instead of considered and constructive.

After a few times of letting this behavior slide, I realized this friend was pushing a boundary. I thought about whether it mattered to me—it did. (I don't like having my feelings dismissed or negated any more than anyone else does; I'm just more likely to let it go for the sake of peace.) When I decided it mattered enough to respond, I messaged her and said, "I notice you frequently dismiss my feelings with social media comments that feel rude. I care about you and respect you, but please understand it isn't okay for you to keep dismissing my feelings either privately or publicly. I'm happy to have you share your opinion even when it differs from mine, but I will not allow you to continue to be dismissive or rude to me."

I was pretty certain that this would be the end of that friendship because in the past, when I've asserted myself as someone who pushes against a firm boundary, I've lost friends. But I also realized I was okay with losing this particular friend because if she couldn't respect my boundaries, she wasn't someone I wanted in my life anyway. So, I was prepared for a negative response. Therefore, I was surprised and delighted when she responded, "I am so sorry. I wasn't trying to be rude or dismissive. Can you help me understand a better way to communicate that doesn't feel that way?" It turned out she was horrified that I felt like she was dismissing me, and she was worried she'd offended others without realizing it because of the way she was saying things.

I learned a lot about boundaries from this experience, and my success in setting and enforcing a seemingly minor boundary gave me a huge confidence boost in enforcing larger and more important ones. Some things this taught me that can benefit you as well:

- If someone is willing to cross your boundaries without care or concern, then they aren't a true friend, and you likely don't need them in your life.

- Your needs are just as valid and important as anyone else's, so it's essential you enforce your boundaries as a form self-compassion.

- When you ask someone to stop violating your boundaries, you aren't responsible for how they react. If they go ballistic, it's likely that they don't want to be in relationship to you anymore, and your life will be better off for their leaving.

- Not enforcing boundaries is a way of attempting to control how another person perceives you, and it's not being authentic to who you are.

- There are polite, compassionate, and loving ways to enforce boundaries.

- Your boundaries don't take away something from someone else.

- Appropriate boundaries can nourish and strengthen relationships.

- Having a boundary isn't selfish; it's a form of self-care.

- Enforcing your boundaries is empowering.

- The more you practice enforcing boundaries, the better you get at it.

Is This Mine?

"Is this mine?" is a simple technique you can use any time you start to have weird physical or emotional feelings and don't recognize the source. I use it as a kind of check-in anytime I recognize I might be having an empathic experience. It's easy to do, and you can even practice it in public—nobody will notice except you.

As soon as you become aware you are having a random emotional or physical symptom that has seemingly come out of nowhere, pause for a minute and ask in your mind, "Is this mine?" Take several deep breaths in through your nose and out through your mouth as you take your figurative internal temperature. I find that when I do this, I can distinguish between those feelings that are actually mine and those that belong to someone else.

When I recognize that a feeling belongs to someone else, I say in my mind, "Thank you for sharing this information with me," and I decide whether it's something I can react to or whether I just need to move on. For instance, if the feeling arises during a psychic or energy healing session, I can be relatively certain it's coming from my clients or healing partner and respond to the information appropriately. If I'm with one of my family members or friends, I can ask compassionate questions or find out if there's a way I can help. However, if I'm at the grocery store surrounded by people, I am less likely to be able to do anything about it, so it's probably best if I move on.

How to Release Empathic Information

As soon as I recognize why I'm receiving empathic information and I've determined how I will react to it, I then release it so it doesn't get stuck in me and deplete my energy. There is never a good reason to carry someone else's emotional and physical experiences with you once you've identified them and decided how you'll respond. To release the empathic information:

1. Express gratitude for receiving it.

2. Say in your mind, "This is not mine. I release it."

3. Visualize white light pouring down from above you through the crown of your head, pouring through your entire body, and pushing the feeling down through your feet and into the earth, where it is neutralized. Alternatively, you can visualize the feeling as a black shadow in your body and visualize the shadow lifting out of you and dissipating into the universe.

Sometimes you may find you're still empathically tied to someone with whom you are no longer in relationship. Maintaining this kind of an energetic tie is never healthy because there's usually a good reason that relationship or friendship ended. Therefore, you may need to do some additional energetic hygiene to disconnect those energetic ties so you can get on with your life and allow them to get on with theirs.

When you notice you are still energetically or empathically tied to someone from a relationship that no longer serves you:

1. Visualize yourself and that person, noticing the strands of energy that stretch from you to them.

2. Visualize a giant pair of scissors cutting those ties between you. As you visualize this, affirm, "I release you into the white light of unconditional love, and I thank you for releasing me."

3. Visualize each of you, no longer tied together, surrounded by healing white light.

Turning Down the Volume

I teach this technique to people as a daily exercise to keep empathic information at bay. However, it still allows you to access the information if you need to. This is an especially good practice to use before you head out into a crowd, but you can also use it as a form of daily emotional energy hygiene.

1. Sit quietly with either your tailbone or your feet flat on the floor.

2. Close your eyes and take several deep breaths in through your nose and out through your mouth.

3. When you feel you've entered a calm and relaxed state, visualize two volume knobs in your head. Label one "Me" and the other "Everyone Else."

4. Visualize turning your volume knob all the way up and the other one all the way down.

5. You can also create custom knobs, such as one labeled "John" if you have a need to tune in to John for some reason (for instance, I do this with my energy healing partners and psychic clients). Adjust accordingly.

This is a powerful and simple technique that's easy to customize for different situations. It's something I practice daily. However, there are a couple of things to keep in mind:

- Initially, you may need to adjust your volume knobs every few hours to keep the visualization working for you. With time, you can set it in the morning and hold it for several hours or even all day. If you notice other people's feelings creeping back in, check in with your volume knobs and reset them.

- If you're using this technique because you're about to head out into a crowd, it's extremely important you set your volume *before* you enter the crowd (for example, if I'm heading into the city, I will check and set my volume switches in the car in a less populous area before I enter the city). I find it's quite difficult to set the volume switches once you're actually in the crowd because you're in a state of sensory overload from everyone's unfiltered feelings.

Additional Techniques for Empaths

You can also use any of the psychic protection techniques listed in chapter 4 to help control your empathic abilities, such as using crystals or putting up a shield. You may also discover other techniques that work well for you, so feel free to experiment— different things work for different people.

· ·

By learning to manage and control your empathic abilities, you'll find it's easier to work with them for the gifts they are instead of experiencing only the challenges associated with empathy. Doing so has brought a lot of peace to the empaths I know, ending years of struggle and creating a more peaceful, joyful, and meaningful life.

CHAPTER 8

Helping Your Psychic Child

· ·

Growing up as a psychic child, I not only didn't know I was psychic but believed, due to societal and religious conditioning, that there was something wrong with the experiences I was having. It wasn't an easy way to be in the world as a child, teen, and young adult, and after I accepted and learned to work with my psychic abilities, I promised myself that if I ever wrote a book about psychic ability, I'd include information for parents, grandparents, aunts, uncles, older siblings, and other adults about how to help psychic kids.

Psychic ability is a natural gift, and children are much more open to psychic sensory information than adults. Why? Because they lack the conditioning to recognize that what they're sensing freaks a lot of people out, and they lack the societal context to be frightened by their experiences. Because of this, typically you'll find that young children—especially toddlers and preschoolers—are open conduits for psychic information until they are conditioned to feel differently (something that often happens by the time they enter kindergarten).

I have vague memories from my pre-K years of all sorts of "imaginary" friends and knowing things I should have had no way of knowing. But by the time I was in school, I actively suppressed or dismissed that intuitive information as being my imagination or something that was not okay to share with others because it scared them and made me "weird." Resultantly, I suppressed and denied my abilities for nearly forty years, leading to anxiety, less-than-ideal life choices, and a lot of unhappiness. All I wanted was to be "normal," but it came at great personal cost.

The adults in a psychic child's life can have a huge influence on how that child experiences their intuitive side. Helping to normalize and accept such experiences can go a long way toward improving their quality of life both while they're a child and as an adult.

IS MY CHILD PSYCHIC?

The first answer to this question is simple: of course your child is psychic. But what the question is really asking is how much access to or awareness of intuitive information your child has. Everyone has access to psychic sensory information, but a combination of factors will determine whether that ability flourishes and grows or the child learns their natural, Source-given abilities are unacceptable and therefore suppresses them. The adults in the child's life will be a major factor in determining which way it goes.

With that being said, in my experience, children in the past four-plus decades have been born with increasingly powerful psychic abilities. We can see signs of this in the generation known as millennials, who were born starting in roughly 1981. For example, people in this generation tend to be more sensitive to the feelings of others, which arises from empathy, and they have been described as indigo children (see the next section). Because the babies born as a part of the millennial generation and the generations coming after them have a more powerful link to Source energy, they have more memories of who they are as souls than older folks do.

Indigo, Rainbow, and Crystal Children

Babies with this increased connection to Source started appearing in the 1960s with the birth of Gen Xers. During this time, these soul-connected babies were so few and far between that there wasn't a discernible pattern. They began to arrive in slightly greater numbers in the 1970s, but it wasn't until the early 1980s that spiritually connected babies began to be born en masse. Recognizing this shift in children, Kryon channel Lee Carroll and energy healer Jan Tober described this group of enlightened children coming to the planet via incarnation as indigo children (so named due to the indigo color they displayed in their auras), and they cowrote the 1999 book *The Indigo Children*. In the book, they outlined the characteristics of what appeared to be a generation ushering in the next evolution of human consciousness. They've written more books since then, and I believe they're essential reading for all parents.

All of these traits arise from their more powerful connection to Source than previous generations. While they still aren't 100 percent aware of who they truly are and where they come from, indigo children have much more remembrance than others. This deeper connection to their spiritual roots is both a source of confidence and a challenge for these young people, who must try to fit within old systems and societies that no longer serve humanity and feel repressive to embodied spirits who are more deeply connected to their soul source.

The entities I channel, the George Collective, have identified the first indigo children and the generations of babies that have come after them as the Fourth Wave of Humanity. They are arriving in large numbers to help humanity make a necessary shift in consciousness.

To that end, the souls entering babies today remember even more than those before them, leading some to classify them as rainbow or crystal children. However, the degree to which they recall who they truly are and their past-life experiences as part of Source energy varies. In general, the evolution is linear, and children born more recently have a deeper recall than those born in the '60s, '70s, and early '80s, but that's a generalization. It varies from person to person, and nurture sometimes trumps nature as children grow into adults, so many are likely to lose or suppress that connection.

So why are they here to help shift consciousness? Many believe they are the generations that will help humanity shed outdated structures, beliefs, and social systems that no longer serve us; in other words, they're here to help us evolve. These spiritually connected young people will take humanity from "me"-focused materialism to "we"-focused spirituality.

Indigo children seem to see the world differently from the generations that came before them. Among their characteristics are:

- A sense of entitlement arising from the remembrance that they come from and are of Source energy
- A highly perceptive nature with enhanced psychic and intuitive abilities
- A desire to awaken others
- A deep sense of social justice and outrage about oppression or unfairness
- A desire to change the world
- Nonmaterialism
- Intolerance for inauthenticity
- An extremely strong-willed nature
- Creativity
- Nonconformism and impatience with the conventional
- Concern and care for the planet and environment
- Truth seeking
- Idealism
- Confidence that, to others, may seem unearned
- Intolerance for rigidity
- Fluidity in traits that previously seemed fixed, such as gender and race
- A disdain for rules
- Being in a hurry to grow up and do something "important"

You can see these traits in the activism of the young in social justice movements such as Occupy Wall Street, LGBTQIA+ rights, and Black Lives Matter. These young people have tremendous potential to bring about necessary and lasting social and spiritual change for humanity, and it's up to the adults in their lives to foster those soulful characteristics instead of suppressing them.

The Psychic Baby and Psychic Toddler

Many newborn babies appear to be wise old souls newly born into a human body. And while babies lack the ability to communicate with formal language, they have in their earliest days, weeks, and months the deepest connection and most powerful remembrance of their time as souls existing in Source energy. They maintain this connection throughout their toddler and preschool years, although it lessens over time as they grow more concerned with human pursuits. It is during this time that toddlers and preschoolers may offer accounts of "back when I was your mom" or other strange tales that may, on the surface, seem like imagination but are probably remembrances of past lives.

My son, Tanner, was a wise old man from the moment he was born. When he was about three, I was snuggled up in bed with him one night when a thought popped into my head. "Tell me about before I was your mom," I said to him.

His little three-year-old face lit up, and he said, "Oohhhhhhh!" as if he'd been waiting his entire short life for me to ask him that question. He proceeded to tell me about being a doctor on a boat to Africa in vivid and surprising detail.

I recall a similar experience when I was about three or four, but with a slightly different outcome. I got out of bed in the middle of the night and went to my parents' bedroom to wake them up.

"I'm ready to go home now," I told them. I was furious when they insisted I was already home because I absolutely knew in my preschool brain I wasn't. My parents were equally frustrated with my ongoing insistence that home was somewhere else.

Signs your baby, toddler, or preschooler is connecting to psychic information include:

- Active and detailed imagination
- Detailed stories or recall about past lives or events in the past they can't possibly know anything about
- Vivid dreams, nightmares, or night terrors
- Staring at a fixed point and babbling, pointing, and laughing
- Imaginary friends
- Saying they're talking to a family member who passed away before they were born
- Seeming wise beyond their years
- Emotional and physical sensitivity
- Talking about seeing angels or religious figures
- Being distractible for their age
- Describing people in energetic terms, such as "Aunt Julie is blue" or "Grandma buzzes"
- Describing other things in energetic terms, such as, "It's Monday, but it feels Friday"
- As babies, being either preternaturally calm or overly fussy

The Psychic Child

As children enter school, they become easily influenced by their peers. Because of this, they may begin to perceive their abilities or differences as isolating. They may begin to feel like they're the "weird kid." In addition, empathic abilities may make them more susceptible to unexplained mood swings and random aches and pains or illnesses.

By the time they've entered about first grade, children whose abilities aren't being encouraged and supported by the adults in their lives have learned that to discuss or share those experiences is socially unacceptable and may even get them into trouble. Because of this, they begin to suppress their abilities as best they can, which can lead to anxiety, behavioral issues, and physical illnesses. They may begin to display behavioral changes that adults tend to diagnose as disorders such as attention deficit hyperactivity disorder (ADHD) or oppositional defiant disorder (ODD).

Some things you might notice with a psychic school-age child include:

- Anxiety
- Social isolation
- Fear of the dark
- Vivid imagination
- Creative expression through writing, music, dance, or visual arts
- Empathy and compassion for other children
- Wisdom that seems beyond their years
- Being "oversensitive" or "overemotional"
- Being easily distracted
- Difficulty sleeping or trouble getting to bed
- Unexplained physical symptoms, particularly headaches and nausea
- Getting strong, unshakeable first impressions upon meeting a new person
- Poor boundaries
- A growing interest in paranormal topics, such as ghosts and UFOs
- A strong affinity for a certain period of history

The Psychic Teen

By the time your child is a teen, chances are the most important thing in their life is fitting in, and that desire can be a powerful force in what they do with their psychic abilities during this time. For example, Tanner told me all he wanted was to be "normal," and so he simply was going to ignore his psychic abilities, period. This is fairly common, so don't be dismayed if this happens. When Tanner told me that, my response was basically, "Okay, you do what you need to. I'm here if you need me."

However, not all teens are the same, and some choose to lean into their abilities instead because they feel so strongly compelled to do so. For example, my daughter-in-law's younger sister Luna is so pulled to her abilities that they have become one of the most important aspects of her life. She's learning everything she can about working with them—something her supportive parents are encouraging her to explore.

Some other things you may notice with psychic teens:

- Questioning authority and why things have always been a certain way and can't be another way

- Developing a fascination with all things paranormal, such as reading books or watching TV shows about paranormal activity and wanting to visit haunted places

- Having vivid dreams and/or sleeping poorly

- Questioning religious teachings and asserting their own version of spirituality

- Exploration of their gender identity and/or sexual orientation

- Anxiety, depression, and unusual mood swings

- Unexplainable physical symptoms or physical illnesses that appear to be undiagnosable or psychosomatic

- Coming home from school or large gatherings exhausted

- Needing a day or two to decompress after a social event

- Experimentation with drugs and alcohol as numbing agents

- Strengthening or awakening of the various clairs

HOW TO SAFELY ENCOURAGE A PSYCHIC CHILD

So, what is an adult's role in their psychic child's development? Perhaps the most important thing you can do is to not treat your child as if their abilities are unusual, frightening, or bad in some way. Instead, try as much as you can to normalize their experiences, allowing them to express what they're noticing without judgment, criticism, or fear.

Allow Them to Share Their Experiences

Listen without judgment to the experiences your child has to share. Ask open-ended, nonleading questions, such as:

"Can you tell me more?"

"How do you feel about that?"

"Why do you think you noticed that?"

Avoid judgmental commentary and instead opt for phrases such as:

"Thank you for trusting me with that."

"What an interesting experience! Thanks for sharing."

If they share a frightening experience, or one that feels frightening to you, don't react with fear. Instead, encourage them to tell you all about it and then ask a question such as "What do you think that was about?," "What about that did you find frightening?," or "How did that make you feel?" Likewise, if they have an "imaginary friend" or describe a person you can't see, don't react fearfully. Instead, ask questions such as "Did they tell you their name?" or "What did they want you to know?"

If your child decides they don't want to deal with their abilities for the time being, allow that as well. Let your child's current beliefs and attitudes guide you as to how best to support them on their psychic journey. When in doubt, it's always okay to ask, "How can I best support you right now?"

Educate Yourself

Educate yourself and other adults in your child's life about psychic ability. If you understand that it's perfectly natural and recognize how it might manifest, then you can help to normalize the experience for your child.

If there's an influential adult in your child's life who doesn't believe in psychic abilities or seems to be making your child feel uncomfortable about their experiences, step in and help them to understand. If that adult refuses to do so, you may wish to limit their exposure to your child or put your foot down and tell them you will not allow them to communicate negatively with your child about their abilities.

Avoid Labels

We tend to be averse to labels in my house because I find them to be limiting. So, while you can help your children find words to express what they're experiencing, you don't need to apply labels to it. Even labels that we deem positive, such as being a "good kid" or a "strong clairvoyant," can create limitations because kids are so impressionable. Allow your child the freedom to create their own self-definition rather than slapping them with a label that they feel they have to live up to or be confined by.

By avoiding labels, you allow your child the freedom to discover who they are as a psychic and as a human being without placing the weight of expectation upon them. Let them lead the way.

Teach Simple Psychic Protection Techniques

Even very young children can learn simple, age-appropriate visualizations and affirmations to protect themselves psychically. This can be a simple, silly rhyme or tongue twister you say with the child whenever they feel frightened or a quick visualization of them surrounded by a big bubble. You can also use objects such as nontoxic crystals—for example, allowing them to wear a shungite bracelet (only with older children who won't try to put crystals in their mouths).

When Tanner started having night terrors at about age three, we made a dream catcher together out of an embroidery hoop, string, and some amethyst and black tourmaline beads. We hung it above his bed, and every night before he went to sleep, we said a simple affirmation: "Tonight I dream of happy things."

You can also empower your child by creating what I like to call "juju spray." To make this, you'll need:

- A small spray bottle
- An amethyst crystal
- Water
- ½ teaspoon of sea salt or Himalayan pink salt
- One to two drops of lavender essential oil

Drop everything into the bottle and shake to mix it up. Your child can spritz some around their room when they are frightened or at night before sleep to keep bad dreams at bay.

For older children, you can teach them simple, age-appropriate meditation techniques. One easy technique is to sit quietly with their eyes closed and visualize colors. Your child can visualize any color they wish, or they can make a slideshow of colors. Make sure meditation sessions only last a few minutes for young children or up to ten minutes for tweens.

Find a Mentor

If you feel ill equipped to help your psychic child, pairing them with an experienced psychic mentor may be extremely helpful as they get older and their abilities grow and mature. Ask a local psychic for recommendations or, if you know someone you trust, see whether that person would be interested in supporting your child. Good community resources include metaphysical and spiritual bookstores, crystal shops, and New Age spirituality centers.

Allow Psychic Play

Playing simple psychic games with your child is another great way to support, encourage, and normalize your child's abilities. Simple matching games are a great option, or you can play simple versions of some of the games described in chapter 6. Make it fun and low stakes; keep sessions short, and be encouraging, even if your child is feeling discouraged or not having a great day. Allow your child to lead the way with these simple games.

Other simple games you can try include:

- Twenty Questions: Say "I'm thinking of a(n) . . ." and give your child a simple category, such as animals, cartoons, or toys. Encourage your child to share their very first impression, and then allow them to ask twenty yes or no questions, guessing after each. Keep it light and fun.

- Guess Which Hand: Place a small item in one of your hands while out of your child's view, then hold out your hands to allow your child to guess which hand the item is in. Encourage them to go with their first instinct.

- What's in the Box?: Place small items in a few different boxes and hand each box to your child. Encourage them to guess what's inside.

- Creative drawing or writing: You can also encourage your child to draw or write the things they see and experience. For example, if they say, "Today feels like a mad day," say, "Can you draw me a picture showing me what you mean?"

- I'm Thinking of: Tell your child, "I'm thinking of a number between one and ten," and give them a few guesses. Take turns so your child can also think of a number.

- I Spy with My Third Eye: Visualize a simple object in your mind, such as a blue ball, a green triangle, or your pet lizard. Say, "I spy with my third eye something that is . . ." and give one defining characteristic. Close your eyes and visualize, and encourage your child to close their eyes to try to see what you do. Take turns being the spy and the guesser.

Encourage Journaling

Encourage your child to keep a simple, age-appropriate journal in which they record their experiences, impressions, and dreams. Find a type of journaling your child enjoys—they could write, record video or audio, or draw pictures and symbols.

Make sure your child knows their journal is safe and you will only look in it if they invite you to do so. Tell them they can record anything they wish, and then respect your child's privacy. Don't ask them to share, but if they offer, be nonjudgmental and respectful in your commentary, asking open ended questions such as "Would you like to tell me more about this?"

··

Be Open

As a parent who raised a psychic child, as well as an adult who grew up as a psychic child, the best piece of advice I can offer you is this: be open. Even if your child's psychic abilities seem strange to you, avoid judgment, encourage conversation, and let them know you're always there if they want to share anything or if they feel they need support. By being open to your child's unique abilities and providing a soft place to land, chances are your child can grow to adulthood with a healthy sense of their psychic abilities as natural, normal, and helpful.

CHAPTER 9

Ethics, Responsibility, and Communication

· ·

I f you've ever watched a television show featuring a
psychic, you may have encountered a scene that goes
a little like this. The psychic is at the grocery store—or
the beauty parlor, a restaurant, or another public venue—
when suddenly they get a psychic "hit" about a random
stranger nearby. Unable to contain themselves, the
psychic goes up to said stranger and starts sharing
the information.

That's TV land, but it's not typically how psychics operate. In fact, randomly approaching a stranger and spewing psychic information, while it makes for good television, isn't necessarily the most ethical use of psychic abilities.

Because the nature of psychic information is often highly personal, it's important that psychics behave ethically with the information they receive. Most working psychics abide by a code of ethics in managing and working with their abilities as well as communicating with others. In this chapter, we'll examine the ethical responsibilities of psychics as well as cover important information about how and when to communicate psychic information.

THE GREATEST GOOD

The first and most important ethical principle for any psychic, energy healer, or someone working in the spiritual arts is to serve the highest and greatest good. Therefore, my first consideration in everything I do is "Does this serve the greatest good?" If it feels like it doesn't, then it is often information coming from ego and not from Source.

There's a lot to unpack in that previous statement, so let's get into it.

What Is the Greatest Good?

The greatest good is a phrase I use interchangeably with *highest and greatest good* or *highest good*. All are ways of saying that the information I receive and share, the choices I make, and the actions I take serve Source energy in ways that align with Source's ultimate goal of experiencing and incarnated souls re-membering (rejoining Source).

Source—sometimes referred to as Spirit, God, Universal Intelligence, the Divine, Christ Consciousness, the Krishna Consciousness, Collective Consciousness, Zero Point Field, the Field, and many other names from various cultures and traditions—is the energy from which we came and to which we will all eventually return. It is a place of pure love and light that is far vaster and more unconditionally loving than we can ever understand with our limited human minds.

Source is All That Is, Was, or Ever Will Be. It existed as an energetic presence in harmony, light, and love, but it had a desire to know itself in new ways. And so, Source created a playground in which it could get to know itself better through new experiences.

You can read a human representation of Source's creation of its playground in the creation stories from cultures and traditions around the world and throughout human history. These stories seek to symbolically represent the springing forth of creation from Source energy, each from the human perspective of understanding of the teachings and traditions of a particular culture. If you study them, you will find there are underlying similarities, although the specifics vary greatly.

Regardless of which creation myth you learned and resonate with, however, the bottom line is similar. Source wished to understand the all of everything, and so it created a place in which it could play with the concepts of duality: of dark and light, love and hate, this and that, here and there, hot and cold, and, of course, of everything in between these poles. In order to do this, Source created a realm where the exploration of each of these aspects was possible and then sent pieces of itself grouped into energetic packets we call souls or consciousnesses into the various kinds of matter: rocks, trees, land, oceans, animals, plants, and people. The ultimate plan with all of these things was to generate experiences of duality so Source could know itself better.

All humans (and indeed everything you perceive on planet Earth with your five physical senses) are made of spiritual consciousness taking physical form. Your energy is the same as the energy of a rock, tree, or dog, for instance. It's all a bundle of Source energy that has agreed to assume a certain physical form in the Earth realm for a period in order to support the overall growth and expansion of Source energy. Some energies have a more visibly active and expressive consciousness than others—for example, souls in human bodies appear to take a more active role in pursing experiences and spiritual growth than the consciousness that makes up something such as a rock—but all forms of Source energy and consciousness contribute to Source energy's desire to experience itself in all possible ways with the ultimate goal of one day re-membering with a full understanding of everything that is, was, and ever will be as well as the spaces of here, there, and in between.

Before each human embodiment, the packet of Source energy known as the soul makes a plan. The plan for each lifetime is what is commonly referred to as *karma*, and it encompasses the major types of experiences the individual soul will have during each period of embodiment, known as an *incarnation* or *life*. You can find a roadmap to the individual karma of a lifetime using practices such as astrological natal charting or personal numerology.

Souls come back time and time and time again (some believe souls each have thousands or tens of thousands of lives) in order to ultimately have every experience in a place of duality. This means that by the time you re-member, sometimes called reaching enlightenment, your soul will have had all experiences available in the playground of duality, and you will have been it all: a beggar and a rich person; a liar and a truth seeker; a murderer and a victim; a sick person and a healer.

However, these plans leave room for the individual choice of the human. While our souls plan the basic karmic elements of our lives as embodied humans, such as the families we are born into, the place we are born, the major challenges we may face, and the opportunities that may arise during our lifetimes, we always have the choice of what we will do with those experiences and how we will respond to them. Therefore, an embodied spirit frequently journeys far from its intended path in a lifetime, and that's perfectly okay because we all eventually find our way back to Source in one way or another. And the experiences we have along the way all allow Source to play, discover, and explore, even if we've wandered off in a direction we never planned before we embodied.

Embodied souls also have the opportunity in the playground to create. We do this through our thoughts, words, actions, and reactions; as we engage in each of these things, we create the experiences we have while embodied.

Creation can be accomplished on an individual level or collectively. Individually, we may create for ourselves things such as prosperity or lack, health or sickness, joy or sadness, and other elements of duality. On a collective level, humanity creates the circumstances that allow events and conditions to arise on a massive scale, such as weather patterns, political events, times of peace and prosperity, pandemics, and more. While some of these events are the unintended consequences of collective creation, they still serve Source's desire to know Itself better. However, the ultimate goal, which is the highest and greatest good, is for individual consciousness to ultimately reach an enlightened place in which all of the packets of Source energy remember that we are of Source and rejoin Source in a state of balance, love, harmony, and joy.

As embodied humans, we don't always see or understand the plans our souls made for us and for universal good when we were still spirits living in Source energy and preparing to become embodied. We may receive glimpses of this overarching plan throughout our lives via psychic information, dreams, and other forms of spiritual guidance, but our overall chosen path for this lifetime isn't something we have detailed recall of in our conscious minds.

So, while all human paths ultimately serve the desire of Source energy to know itself better, the greatest good is the path that leads to growth and re-membering with Source energy. And the thing that almost always leads us away from enlightenment is the uniquely human quality called ego.

Ego and the Greatest Good

One thing that sets the human soul apart from packets of Source energy taking other forms is the presence of "I," also known as ego. Ego is a function of the human body and mind; it is of the body and not of the soul. It's like a filter placed over our soul that creates the individual experience of "I" and "me," while filtering out the remembrance of self as Source energy.

Ego serves an important purpose in allowing us to become fully immersed in the experience of being an embodied human. It also allows us to differentiate ourselves from everything else, which is necessary for experiencing duality and living out our karma for a set lifetime.

Ego is neither inherently bad nor good. It is simply a mechanism that allows us to immerse fully into the human experience. However, as embodied spirits, we have the opportunity to choose to allow ego to control us or to choose to control our egos. When our egos control us, we are more likely to act without awareness, which usually brings unintended results—for example, a world leader being controlled by ego might wage war out of the desire for power, control, and dominion over land, possessions, and people. A world leader who is in control of ego might instead seek cooperation, peace, and harmony for all in order to create a better world. Unfortunately, it's not always easy to notice when ego is in control, and it's very easy to allow your ego to control you from time to time. Even the most enlightened souls I know sometimes slip into ego-driven choices and behaviors.

So, what does this have to do with receiving psychic information and serving the greatest good? Simply this: when you are acting from ego, you aren't serving the greatest good. It's an easy trap to fall into as a psychic.

Suppose a psychic medium is doing a gallery reading in which they stand before a large audience communicating messages from dead loved ones. As someone who has been onstage frequently as a speaker (although I've never done gallery readings—mainly because I know my ego would get involved), I know how much pressure I receive from my ego to "do a good job" as I speak. So, there's our fictional psychic, standing on stage ready to deliver messages from loved ones and under tremendous pressure from their ego to "get it right." They close their eyes, take a deep breath, and receive nothing. Their mind is a complete blank. However, when they open their eyes and look out at the audience, they see all the hopeful faces ready to receive messages of love from lost friends and family. The psychic's ego quietly whispers, "They're waiting. You can't tell them you've got bupkis."

And so, our medium, under pressure from their ego, starts to speak using cold reading techniques and piggybacking on the responses from the audience instead of sharing genuine information they are receiving from Source. The audience is none the wiser. They walk away believing they have received messages of love and comfort, but all they've heard is information from the medium's mind and ego.

At this point, many ask, "If they feel better, what's the harm?" It's a cogent argument, but it's also a slippery slope. One such incident may turn into more until a genuine psychic who originally started with the intent to serve the greatest good instead is defrauding people in order to serve their ego. They have become a slave to their ego, which will further hamper their ability to provide genuine information that serves the highest good.

While the medium's response in such a situation is understandable (social pressure is a powerful motivator), the party trick of cold reading is not serving the greatest good. And even if their intention is that the cold reading techniques trigger genuine information from Spirit, it's dishonest and unfair to the participants who have come to receive genuine information.

With all that being said, however, I totally understand the urge. While it's extremely rare, occasionally in a reading I receive absolutely no information. It's embarrassing to admit that to my client, who has come to me for a reason. However, when it does happen, I explain it to my client right away. Then, I offer options such as drawing cards to see whether we can kick-start the process, rescheduling, or returning the money they paid for the reading. I try at all times in my work as a psychic and energy healer to remain in control of my ego so I can truly serve the greatest good.

So how can you recognize ego at play? Let's take a look at a few common signs your ego is in control:

- You feel fear

- You act from pressure to perform instead of from genuine information

- You act from a desire for others to like you or be impressed by you

- You attempt to control others or receive personal gain through the information you share

- The information you receive feels limiting instead of expansive

- You're only in it for the money

- You're worried you'll fail

- You feel judgmental or critical about your client or the information you receive

- You feel you must interpret the information you're receiving instead of sharing it as it comes

- You feel as if you must get everything in a reading 100 percent right

- If your client doesn't validate the information you share, you seize up or try to find a way to share it that they will validate

- You are unwilling to share or report some piece of information (such as my pornstache example in chapter 3) because it feels in some way inappropriate

- You steer the information in a direction you find pleasing instead of offering it exactly as you receive it

PROFESSIONAL AND PERSONAL INTEGRITY AND ETHICS

While greatest good should always be your main ethical principle, there are other boundaries you need to keep in mind as you work with psychic information, particularly if you work with clients.

- Always keep information in a psychic reading confidential.

- If you receive information that could truly be harmful, such as a date of death, it's best to not share it. (In my experience, these usually come from ego instead of Source anyway.)

- Only consciously read someone with their permission. Sometimes you may randomly receive psychic information, but you can use shielding techniques to shut it down so you don't invade someone else's privacy. Everyone is entitled to their own psychic privacy unless they actively seek a psychic reading.

- Only share psychic information with people if they've indicated a willingness to receive it.

- Treat all clients with respect and care regardless of race, religion, ethnicity, gender identification, sexual orientation, or other parts of their identity.

- If you are unable to set aside a personal prejudice about client, refund their money and refer them to a different psychic.

- Never provide a medical diagnosis, prescribe treatment, or countermand a doctor's orders.

- Refer clients who need it to medical and psychological professionals.

- Never take someone's money under false pretenses.

- Follow your client's need. If they feel uncomfortable or wish to stop receiving information, immediately comply with their wishes.

- If you are unable to connect during a reading, be honest about it and offer multiple options for your client.

- Remain in a space of unconditional love, compassion, openness, and allowing. If you are unable to achieve such a state before a reading, reschedule your client or refund their money (psychics have bad days, too).

- Never guarantee accuracy. No psychic is right 100 percent of the time, so you should never represent that you are.

- Behave in a professional manner when working with clients.

- Don't research your client online before you speak to them in order to obtain information that will "assist" in your reading.

- If you read professionally, follow all best business practices including obtaining appropriate business licenses and permits, reporting income, and paying taxes.

CONFIDENTIALITY

While I've already mentioned confidentiality, it's so important that I want to highlight it further here. Maintaining client confidentiality is, after serving the greatest good, the single most important ethic a psychic should follow.

- Never share a client's personal information without permission—not even with friends or family.

- If you wish to use someone's story as an example when you're writing or speaking about your work, change identifying information and details so the information is anonymous.

- If someone else is in the room when you're doing a phone or online reading, always disclose to the client that that person is present and ask whether it's okay. If it's not, then ask the person to leave the room or go into another room yourself. If that's not possible, reschedule the reading.

COMMUNICATION SKILLS FOR PSYCHICS

Everyone has their own communication style, and it's okay to inject your personality into your psychic work. However, it's also essential to understand best practices for communication skills in order to remain open and clear, and offer professional communication at all times.

- Explain your process and what your client can expect at the outset of a session. Tell them about any tools you might use and why you use them, and ask whether they have any questions before you begin.

- If you have any quirks that may come out while you're doing a reading—for example, I frequently pause and look up and to the left when I'm doing a reading because that is where my information seems to come from—explain that before you start so your client expects it.

- At the outset of a reading, ask the client how they would like to proceed: would they prefer to ask questions, are they seeking a back-and-forth conversation, or would they rather you share all the information you receive without providing feedback?

- Report what you see, hear, feel, and experience exactly as it comes to you. Don't try to interpret it or make it more palatable for your client.

- If something is foggy or hazy, make sure you let your client know that.

- If you see something you are unable to understand, describe it as best as possible, but tell the client honestly that you don't know what it means or exactly what you are communicating.

- If your client wishes to share information, practice deep listening skills so you can truly understand what they're trying to tell you.

- If you don't know the answer to a question your client asks, be honest about it.

- If a client is unable to confirm information you share, tell them that maybe it doesn't relate to them at all or they might understand it more later, and then move on. Don't force information that your client isn't ready to receive or that truly doesn't resonate with them.

- Avoid swearing, crass language, rude jokes, and any language that could be interpreted as racist, sexist, or culturally inappropriate. If a spirit you are communicating with uses such language, then warn the client, ask whether they want to hear the exact worded message, and share it if so. Occasionally, spirits will communicate in this way in order to confirm it's actually them.

- No matter how random a piece of information seems, share it. You never know what will trigger a remembrance in your client of something integral to their growth and development.

- Warn clients about ten minutes before the end of the session that your time is almost up and allow them to ask any remaining questions they may have.

Although I make every effort to set aside ego in my psychic work, it still comes to my very human mind, which is overlaid with filters arising from my personal perceptions, beliefs, cultural background, experiences, expectations, prejudices, preferences, and communication styles. When I receive psychic information, it filters down through all of these aspects before it reaches the person I'm reading, and the same goes for every psychic on the planet. Therefore, each psychic is a unique individual who receives and shares information in a manner that is different from every other person.

Because of this, psychics don't always "click" with every person seeking psychic information. This is an extremely important concept to understand in psychic communication, because if the energy and chemistry is off in a relationship between a person sharing psychic information and the person receiving it, then there's a good chance the information will either be poorly communicated or poorly received. It's perfectly fine for psychics and their clients to admit the chemistry isn't quite right and for clients to seek someone whom they vibe with. Not everyone is everyone else's cup of tea, and if you don't connect with someone else, it says nothing negative about either of you as long as you are willing to part ways with compassion.

However, whether you work professionally as a psychic or you engage your psychic abilities strictly for personal guidance or to share with friends and family, it's important you remain in an ethical, loving, and helpful space with the intention of serving the greatest good. It's also necessary to be aware of the various manifestations of ego and how that may affect your work as a psychic in order to truly support the highest good of the universe.

Put Your Psychic Abilities to Work in Your Life

··

There is no exact blueprint for being a psychic. Everyone receives and perceives information in their own ways, and the information is always filtered through the personal experiences and ego of the psychic who receives and delivers it. Because of this, everyone's psychic experience is different, and this is by design. Our individual quirks as human beings contribute to the whole of Source's goal to experience Itself. Even when we wander far afield from our originally intended paths, we are still contributing to that overall purpose with our uniquely human experiences.

Because you have free will, you get to decide whether you engage your psychic abilities or ignore them. You also get to determine how much of a role your abilities play in your life and whether you're willing to follow the guidance you receive or if you'd rather do something entirely different. Choosing to embrace your psychic abilities can be empowering, but in order to allow their fullest and most meaningful expression in your life, it's helpful to understand how you receive and perceive them—and to find ways to manage them and tools to help so they work for you.

Messages from Spirit always exist to serve our greatest good, but often we lack the understanding to work with them to guide us in a positive direction. Instead, we fight against them, to our own detriment. The psychic journey is always a part of the human journey, so ultimately each individual has the opportunity to decide what the information means to us, how big of a role it plays in our lives, and how we can best use it to support us as we walk our path.

I can't tell you what role your psychic experiences should play in your life, but I can share my own sentiments. As I've mentioned throughout this book, I spent many years using my cultural and religious conditioning as a reason to push away my intuitive nature. And while that period in my life was rich with experiences that led me to where I am today, when I truly decided to step into my power as a psychic being, my life shifted in ways I couldn't have imagined when I was afraid of being perceived as different or unloved because of my true nature.

Since leaning into my abilities, I have walked a more joyful, insightful, and authentic path. It's true that there are still people in my life who don't approve of or believe in my abilities. In the past, I would have used their thoughts and opinions about me to knock me down and as an excuse to remain disempowered. However, what I finally realized is that I can't control the narrative that others create about me, and either I can seek my own truth and joy through being my authentic self or I can let others dictate to me how they think I should live my life.

I made my choice many years ago, and I've never looked back. In making that choice, I discovered that some relationships no longer served me, and I was able to let them go with love. I also realized that other people in my life weren't able to hear or accept my truth, and that's okay as well. I can still love them and maintain my relationships with them while letting them decide who they want to be in relationship with: it's up to them to choose whether they want to know all of me or simply engage with the parts of me that make them comfortable. Either way, I am going to be exactly who I am both inside and outside of those relationships. Their experience of me is their choice, and my experience is mine.

Psychic abilities are gifts from Source. The journey of the psychic is one of personal empowerment. Stepping onto a psychic path provides you with the opportunity to find the ways you can best serve the highest good for you, for others, and for all of humanity and Source energy.

Having psychic ability is also both a privilege and a responsibility, and it's up to you to choose what type of steward you will be of your gifts. You get to decide whether you'll ignore and deny your abilities, use them for personal guidance, or turn to them as a means of connection to Source energy that helps others and serves the greatest good. It's up to you to choose your own personal ethics surrounding your psychic abilities as well as to determine which tools you use, how you communicate your gifts, and whether you share them with others or keep them to yourself.

Nobody can tell you how to live your life or engage your psychic gifts, so my best suggestion is this: go with what feels right to you for as long as it feels right. If it stops feeling right, then pivot and do something else. If you feel good—happy, peaceful, engaged, joyful, free, loving—then you're probably on the path that serves your greatest good. If you feel bad—unhappy, angry, resentful, disengaged, trapped, envious, hateful, frightened—then you're likely on a path that doesn't serve you.

Engage in the flow of life using your intuition as a guide and understanding that you never have to remain on a path you've taken simply because you started it. It's always okay to turn back or take another path if you feel guided to do so. In this way, the universe has your back and always provides you with the guidance you need if you are open to receiving it.

In the grand scheme of things, the choice of how you engage your psychic ability is always yours. When you return to Source energy at the end of this incarnation, you will not be judged by whether you chose to follow psychic guidance or ignored it altogether. Instead, you'll be welcomed Home and held in the loving, joyful, peaceful, and compassionate embrace of Source energy until you're ready to return to a human body and do it all over again.

Resources for Psychics

· ·

Below you'll find some helpful resources that will allow you to learn more about and explore the various concepts we've discussed in the pages of this book.

DIVINATION

The Ultimate Guide to Divination: The Beginners Guide to Using Cards, Crystals, Runes, Palmistry, and More for Insight and Predicting the Future by Liz Dean (Fair Winds Press)

PALMISTRY

The Art and Science of Hand Reading: Classical Methods for Self-Discovery through Palmistry by Ellen Goldberg and Dorian Bergen (Destiny Books)

A Little Bit of Palmistry: An Introduction to Palm Reading by Cassandra Eason (Sterling Ethos)

I CHING

The I Ching or Book of Changes: A Guide to Life's Turning Points by Brian Browne Walker (St. Martin's Essentials)

The Everyday I Ching by Sarah Dening (St. Martin's Griffin)

The I Ching or Book of Changes by Richard Wilhelm (Princeton University Press)

RUNES

Runes: Unlock the Secret of the Stones (Running Press, book plus rune set)

The Book of Runes, 25th Anniversary Edition by Ralph H. Blum (Thomas Dunne Books)

TAROT

The Ultimate Guide to Tarot: A Beginner's Guide to the Cards, Spreads, and Revealing the Mystery of the Tarot by Liz Dean (Fair Winds Press)

The Ultimate Guide to Tarot Spreads: Reveal the Answer to Every Question About Work, Home, Fortune, and Love by Liz Dean (Fair Winds Press)

The Rider Tarot Deck by Edward Arthur Waite and Pamela Colman Smith (US Games and Systems Inc.)

The Osho Zen Tarot by Osho and Ma Deva Padma (St. Martin's Press)

NUMEROLOGY

The Ultimate Guide to Numerology: Use the Power of Numbers and Your Birthday Code to Manifest Money, Magic, and Miracles by Tania Gabrielle (Fair Winds Press)

The Complete Idiot's Guide Numerology Workbook: Reveal Essential Truths about Yourself, Your Loved Ones, and the World around You by Patricia Kirkman and Katherine Gleason (Alpha)

ASTROLOGY

LoveToKnow Astrology (horoscopes.lovetoknow.com)

The Only Astrology Book You'll Ever Need by Joanna Martine Woolfolk (Taylor Trade Publishing)

DREAM INTERPRETATION & PSYCHIC SYMBOLS

The Dream Interpretation Handbook: A Guide and Dictionary to Unlock the Meanings of Your Dreams by Karen Frazier (Althea Press)

The Dream Interpretation Dictionary: Symbols, Signs, and Meanings by JM DeBord (Visible Ink Press)

The Book of Psychic Symbols: Interpreting Intuitive Messages by Melaine Barnum (Llewellyn Publications)

Dream Moods Dream Dictionary (DreamMoods.com)

ONLINE PSYCHIC GAMES

Institute of Noetic Sciences (noetic.org)

ESP Championship (psychicscience.org/esp2)

RESOURCES FOR PARENTS

The Indigo Children: The New Kids Have Arrived by Lee Carroll and Jan Tober (Hay House)

The Children of Now by Meg Blackburn Losey, PhD (Weiser)

The Indigo Children: Ten Years Later by Lee Carroll and Jan Tober (Hay House)

REFERENCES

Bem, Darryl. "Feeling the Future: Experimental Evidence for Anomalous Retroactive Influences on Cognition and Affect." *Journal of Personality and Social Psychology*. 2011.

CERN. "The Higgs Boson." n.d. Accessed September 12, 2020. https://home.cern/science/physics/higgs-boson.

Emoto, Masaru. *The Hidden Messages in Water*. New York: Simon and Schuster, 2011.

Howell, Elizabeth. "What Is the Big Bang Theory?" Space.com. November 7, 2017. https://www.space.com/25126-big-bang-theory.html.

Hunt, Tam, and Jonathan Schooler. "The 'Easy Part' of the Hard Problem: A Resonance Theory of Consciousness." *Authorea*. January 4, 2019. https://doi.org/10.22541/au.154659223.37007989

MacDonald, Fiona. 2019. "Scientists Just Unveiled the First-Ever Photo of Quantum Entanglement." ScienceAlert. July 13, 2019. https://www.sciencealert.com/scientists-just-unveiled-the-first-ever-photo-of-quantum-entanglement.

Ornes, Stephen. "The Quantum World Is Mind-Bogglingly Weird." Science News for Students. September 14, 2017. https://www.sciencenewsforstudents.org/article/quantum-world-mind-bogglingly-weird.

Peña, Jonatan. "The Sympathy of Two Pendulum Clocks: Beyond Huygens' Observations." *Scientific Reports*, 6. 2006. https://doi.org/10.1038/srep23580.

Schwartz, Gary E. "William James and the Search for Scientific Evidence of Life after Death." *Journal of Consciousness Studies*. 2010.

Schwartz, Gary E., and William L. Simon. *The Afterlife Experiments: Breakthrough Scientific Evidence of Life After Death*. New York: Simon and Schuster, 2002.

Wilczek, Frank. 2016. "Entanglement Made Simple." *Quanta Magazine*. April 28, 2016. https://www.quantamagazine.org/entanglement-made-simple-20160428.

ACKNOWLEDGMENTS

My education as a psychic has not occurred in a bubble. I've been blessed to work with a number of mentors, teachers, and friends who have all contributed to the work I do. I'm grateful to my psychic friends Seth Michael, AurorA, Luis Navarrete, Tristan David Luciotti, Karen Anderson, William Becker, Jason and Carolyn Masuoka, Mackenna Long, and many others with whom I've been lucky enough to work and learn from over the years.

I'd also like to thank my good friends in the Salty Lil Beaches who have kept me sane, especially the Mom Party Van members Kristen Grey and Kasci Lawrence, as well as my husband Jim, my kids Tanner and Liz, and my daughter-in-law Abby. I'm also grateful to Paula Nuspl, who has been my sounding board and an eager student and friend. Likewise, I'm so thankful for all my healing partners, clients, friends, and readers who have allowed me to work with them to share the craft of psychic work and energy healing. I'm deeply and consciously awed that the George Collective has been with me since the beginning and, I suspect, for every walk I take in a human body.

Finally, thanks to my good friends Cheryl Knight-Wilson and Chad Wilson of *Paranormal Underground* Magazine. Without you two, I would never have started writing about my work. And to everyone at Fair Winds Press, especially Jill Alexander, who was willing to give me a shot at sharing about my life as a psychic.

ABOUT THE AUTHOR

KAREN FRAZIER is a psychic medium, medical intuitive, energy healer, sound healer, spiritual coach, channel, metaphysical parapsychologist, ordained minister, and teacher. She is the author of multiple books and articles about metaphysics, psychic phenomena, crystal healing, energy healing, dream interpretation, and the paranormal.

A frequent guest in the media discussing personal empowerment through energy-healing techniques, Karen has spoken and taught classes at conferences and symposia throughout the Pacific Northwest and appeared on numerous internet and terrestrial radio shows as well as television shows and documentaries such as *The List*, *Life to Afterlife: The Healers*, and *All Around Us*. She teaches classes in psychic development, dream interpretation, energy healing, crystal healing, personal development, and metaphysical healing.

Karen is a columnist for *Paranormal Underground* magazine, writing about psychic phenomena, energy healing, dream interpretation, and metaphysics. She is also the creator and cohost of the *Intention Is Everything Podcast* and the former host and producer of *Paranormal Underground Radio*.

She is a Reiki master-teacher and an ordained minister for the International Metaphysical Ministry. She holds a bachelor of metaphysical science (BMSc) and a master's of metaphysical science (MMSc) as well as a PhD in metaphysical parapsychology. She is currently working on her doctoral dissertation focusing on sound as a source of spiritual healing in order to earn her doctorate of divinity (DD) in spiritual healing. Learn more at AuthorKarenFrazier.com.

ABOUT THE ILLUSTRATOR

ROBERTA ORPWOOD is an internationally published visionary artist and multidisciplinary therapist, focusing her Heart-centred offerings upon Shamanic Soul Medicine Paintings, Shamanic Integrative Therapy, and Sound Healing. Her SoulBird Art Studio and Therapy Practice resides in London, U.K., where all the magic happens.

She specializes in watercolors and is well known for her mastery of color and vibrancy. The inspiration for her art stems from her practice of Shamanic living which includes creating sacred space for ritual and ceremony, communing with Spirit, and acknowledging that everything in this world possesses a spiritual essence, animated and alive (animism).

Her intention is to birth healing artworks that serve as medicine for the soul and psyche. The foundation of Roberta's paintings is to gift the viewer with the opportunity to engage, reflect, and therefore bring to light what needs to be seen, recognized, heard, and, ultimately, healed.

You will find not only Shamans and Ancestors within her creations but also Medicine Women, Spirit Animals, Goddesses, and Spirits of Nature, all interwoven with themes of love, connection, healing and truth.

www.soulbirdart.com

INDEX